PARAMAHAMSA
A Vedantic Tale

PARAMAHAMSA

A Vedantic Tale

R. Subramony

D.K. Printworld (P) Ltd.
Publishers of Indian Traditions

Cataloging in Publication Data — DK
[Courtesy: D.K. Agencies (P) Ltd. <docinfo@dkagencies.com>]

Raja, 1976-
Paramahamsa : a Vedantic tale / R. Subramony.
p. cm.
Includes bibliographical references (p.).
ISBN 13: 9788124605660
ISBN 10: 8124605661

1. Vedanta. 2. Hinduism — India — Tamil Nadu. I. Title.

DDC 181.48 22

ISBN 13: 978-81-246-0566-0 ISBN 10: 81-246-0566-1
First published in India in 2011

Published and printed by:
D.K. Printworld (P) Ltd.
Regd. Office: 'Srikunj', F-52, Bali Nagar
Ramesh Nagar Metro Station
New Delhi – 110 015
Phones: (011) 2545 3975, 2546 6019; *Fax*: (011) 2546 5926
E-mail: indology@dkprintworld.com
Website: www.dkprintworld.com

Dedicated to

- Late Dr Vishnu Bhat (Madras Christian College), an *acharya* of the highest order
- Dr Uma Devi (Trivandrum), who taught me Vedanta and sowed the seeds for this book
- Prof. Leela Subramoni (Trivandrum), a great teacher of English Literature and devotee of Bhagavan Ramana Maharshi
- Late Prof. K. Swaminathan, a prince among men of letters and a spiritual giant
- Chander Prakash Khatri (Umerkot, Sind, Pakistan), who, by asking questions on Hinduism, forced me to read a lot on it
- Dr Kapil Kapoor (JNU), who has created a *parampara* of students of Sanskrit Poetics and Indian tradition
- Dr Makarand Paranjape (JNU), who told me that writing is a *sadhana*
- Vidyaratnam Ramasubramania Dikshitar, a rare Pandit
- Sivayoganandji of Chinmaya Mission, Madurai, who is teaching me Sankara
- Prof. Sankarasubramanian (Ramani), who brought me to Madura College, my second home.

Foreword

HINDUISM, or more accurately, Sanatana Dharma, has been the religion of the land called as Bharat. It has been called by the Chinese as "Yindu" and India by Europeans for centuries. When Akhand Bharat, which included today's Iran [thence came Kaikeyi], Afghanistan [the land of Gandhari and Shakuni] and Pakistan on the west, and Burma and Sri Lanka on the east and south, was 100 percent of Hindu religionists, India was a humane, civilised nation of great economic and scientific achievements.

Fire-worshipping Persians escaping Islamic invasion and brutality came to Gujarat and were treated as honoured fellow citizens. Persecuted Jews came to Mumbai and Kochi and only in India they were welcomed and without any persecution allowed to freely practise their non-proselytising religion in synagogues built for them. So too were Islamic Arabs and European Christians welcomed in Kerala.

This was India before the sequential foreign invasions by uncivilised hordes [such as of Mohammed Ghauri] and dregs of society [such as Robert Clive]. The 1000 years of foreign rule (800 by the Muslims and 200 by the British) has left us all with bitter memories which should now be constructively converted into a resolve to never again allow this to happen.

The Islamic invasion of India resulted in large-scale destruction and vandalisation of Hindu temples, and brutality and imposition of Jaziya (religious tax) on non-Muslim subjects. Alberuni, who accompanied Mohammed Ghazni, has recorded the destruction of Hindu temples by his Islamic invaders. Babar destroyed Ramjanmabhumi temple while Aurangazeb destroyed Mathura and the Viswanath temple in Kashi by issuing a *firman*.

But the fact remains, that everywhere else, such as Iran, Iraq and Egypt, Islamic invasion led to complete conversion of the local population to Islam within a few decades. Same is true of Europe after Christian invasion. But even after 1000 years of brutal rule of Muslim [800 years] and Christian invaders [200 years], undivided India, in 1947, had remained a 75 per cent Hindu majority country. This is because Hindu revolt never ceased till freedom came in 1947. The Vijayanagara kings fought the Muslim Badshahs and ruled over vast areas of India for 300 years to usher in a Hindu renaissance. Chhatrapati Shivaji challenged and stemmed the Islamic tide of the Mughals so much so that had the British not come, the Mahrattas would have liberated India from Islamic rule in early nineteenth century and restored Hindu Rashtra.

After Independence in 1947, in the name of a distorted secularism, the Left-leaning Jawaharlal Nehru and his chosen Marxist historians gave legitimacy to the British version of our history which covertly gave vent to their anti-Hindu feelings in Government textbooks. Hence, time has arrived to re-write these history books purged of the biased version of British Imperialists and coloured by Marxists.

Paramahamsa by Shri R. Subramony is one such research about the unique glory of our Hindu tradition. Bharatha Varsha has witnessed a succession of sages who have preserved the continuity of the eternal message of Sanatana Dharma. It is interesting to learn from the book that Shri Subramony has focused on such sages and scholars who migrated from the Vijayanagara Empire in the wake of the Islamic conquest, to the villages near the Thamirabarani River and contributed to

Vedantic studies. A major focus of the book is on Śaṅkara and his unifying vision of Bharatha Varsha. The contributions of the Kashmiri Pandits have also been dealt with. Kashmir was created by Rishi Kashyapa and is an inseparable part of our Hindu identity, and the plight of Kashmiri Hindus must concern all of us from Kanyakumari and Nicobar to Karakoram and Kashgar.

I hope therefore *Paramahamsa* will serve to awaken the Hindu in order to face the challenges of our time and help us emerge as a Brihad Virat Hindu society in which we will welcome all Muslims and Christians who proudly acknowledge that their ancestors too were Hindus and hence share a common culture and history. That is my concept of Hindustan. I therefore wish the author and the book the best.

Dr Subramanian Swamy
National President, Janata Party

Former Minister of Commerce, Law & Justice
Union Government of India

Preface

PARAMAHAMSA — A Vedantic Tale explores the relevance of Acharya Sankara and Acharya Abhinavagupta to our times. The philosophy of Abhinavagupta and the uniqueness of Kashmiri Shaivism are extensively dealt with through the discourse of the imaginary character Paramahamsa Shivahari, whose *guru* was an expert in *Tantraloka*. This book also throws light on the teachings of Bhagavan Ramana Maharshi and several aspects of Vedanta. The contributions of Sanskrit *pandit*s like Neelakanta Dikshitar, Appaya Dikshitar and Sadasiva Brahmendra who fled from Vijayanagara in the wake of Islamic invasion to the villages near Thamirabarani River in Tirunelveli district, Tamil Nadu are described. It is to be recalled here that Krishna Deva Raya was the king of the mighty Vijayanagara Empire exactly 500 years ago in 1509. It was a great pleasure for me to travel to villages on the banks of the Thamirabarani River like Pallamadai, Kodaganallur and Melacheval where a few *pandit*s still reside. This book can also be regarded as a tribute to the Thamirabarani River along whose banks great scholars resided for centuries. The imaginary narrator of the novel comes to Madurai in the last decade of the twentieth century to study the works of Acharya Sankara and Ramana Maharshi. He is recovering from the shock of the death of both his wife and daughter. He also studies the life of his ancestor, Subbiah who travelled with Paramahamsa Shivahari (both fictitious characters) to different places in the 1860s. Through the conversations of Sankara Shastri, at the beginning of the book, to the narrator and later in the work

Shivahari to Subbiah certain misconceptions regarding the philosophy of Acharya Sankara, especially the false charge that he preached *mayavada*, are cleared. The underlying principle of the novel is the relevance of Advaita Vedanta — non-duality — to our times. Acharya Sankara's philosophy is also explained and its eternal validity is stated. Advaita Vedanta contains the answer to *duhkha* or suffering. *Paramahamsa* is essentially a metaphysical novel and follows the Sanskritic tradition — *Mahabharata* and *Ramayana* for instance — in which focus is more on values and not on the colour of the shirt of a character and ornate descriptions. The contributions of saints such as Tirumular, Vallalar and Kumaraguruparar are described. There are descriptions of *mandapams* (small constructions for pilgrims to take rest), *chatrams* (choultries), *chaturveda mangalams* (villages given as grant for Vedic studies) and the Vedic culture of the 1860s which was on the decline when the colonial power introduced English education in the cities. The reader can get from the book information about the Upanishads and their significance. A major part of the book deals with Kashmir. Kashmir was a major centre of learning before it fell to the Islamic sword in the fourteenth century. There was an intellectual and cultural renaissance in Takshashila (modern Taxila in Pakistan) which spread to Kashmir. India has always been religiously and culturally one. Some scholars from the south visited Kashmir 1000 years ago in search of knowledge. The glory of the past of Madurai and the Meenakshi Temple are also described in the book. Through the travels of Paramahamsa Shivahari and Subbiah we are taken on a journey to the cultural and philosophical heritage of south India. There are conversations between the imaginary twentieth-century descendant of Subbiah and his intellectual opponents. They inform us about how we have neglected the study of our cultural and spiritual heritage after Independence and also how colonialism has uprooted us from our roots. The significance of the Hindu way of thinking in sharp contrast to the West is also highlighted. The book also contains information on *Sri-Vidya upasana* and *kundalini yoga*.

Paramahamsa seeks to focus on the relevance of Upanishadic India in our times. It will also be useful to spiritual seekers, who want to know about Advaita, Acharya Sankara and Acharya Abhinavagupta, Bhagavan Ramana Maharshi and the saints of the Advaitic tradition like Sadashiva Brahmendra. The novel is a window to ancient Indian wisdom; to the perennial philosophy and its eternal relevance. André Malraux said to Jawaharlal Nehru, "Let the great Sankaracharya guide India." This is also the central message of the book.

I am grateful to Dr Subramanya Swamy, President of the Janata Party and former Union Law Minister, for providing the foreword. May God Almighty grant him a long life to serve Sanatana Dharma! I am grateful to Dr Kapil Kapoor (from JNU) for allowing me to quote excerpts from his keynote address delivered on 18 February 2001 at the National Seminar on Decolonising English Education, Department of English, North Gujarat University, Patan (Gujarat, India). I wish to thank Shri V.S. Ramanan, President, for granting me permission to quote from the books about Bhagavan Ramana Maharshi published by Ramanasramam, Tiruvannamalai, Tamil Nadu, especially from *Moments Remembered: Reminiscences of Bhagavan Ramana* by V. Ganesan. I would like to thank the staff of the library of Adi Sankara Nilayam, Veliyanad, Ernakulam district in Kerala run by Chinmaya International Foundation. Thanks are also due to the staff of Chinmaya Mission library in Madurai. The library of Ramakrishna Mutt in Madurai contains a good collection of books on Vedanta and I would like to thank the Head of the Sri Ramakrishna Mutt, Madurai, Swami Kamalathmananda for allowing me to use them. Swamiji has taken personal initiative in buying more books for the library. I thank Smt Hema, librarian of Madura College, Madurai, for her valuable suggestions for the book. She is widely read in philosophy and literature. The Victora Edward Hall Library in Madurai also possesses a rare collection which was useful to me. I thank my colleague Dr R. Raja who is responsible for my interest in Shaiva Siddhanta. Visiting frequently one of the rarest of rare *pandit*s Vidyaratnam Ramasubramania Dikshitar of Suttamali village gave me an idea of how scholars lived in the olden days. I will always be grateful to him for his hospitality and encouragement. The Yajnavalkya Mutt of Melacheval village contains rare manuscripts and palm leaves of the Vijayanagara period. I thank Shri Ganapati Iyer, who is taking care of the Mutt, for allowing me access to them. I also thank Dr Subbulakshmi Sundaram for reading the manuscript and pointing out errors. I would also like to thank Shri Susheel K. Mittal who runs D.K. Printworld for accepting my book for publication. Most publishers these days will not agree to publish a serious book like this.

1

In Madurai where Goddess Meenakshi reigned as the warrior queen and later as the fish-eyed beloved of Lord Sundareshvara, I have decided to spend the third of the four *ashramas* — *vanaprastha* — of my life. It is a blessed spot where Indra expiated his sins after having slain an innocent demon; where the Naicker king built the huge Meenakshi shrine after it was demolished by the Sultans; where the Sangam scholars deliberated in divine Tamil and tested the literary merit of their work on the golden lotus pond; where Manikkavacakar and Appar sang in praise of Lord Shiva.

As Sri Sankara says in the opening verse of the *Saundarya-Lahari*:

> *shivah shaktyayukto yadi bhavati shaktah prabhavitum* ।
> *na cedevam devo na khalu kusalah spanditum api* ॥

> Shiva is able to create only when he is united with Shakti;
> if not thus, the God cannot even move.

I survey the temple towers every morning at *brahma-muhurtta*, recalling the ancient Tamil poetic work of the Sangam Age, the *Madurai Kaanchi*:

> The poet enters the city by its great gate, the posts of which are carved with images of goddess Lakshmi and which is grimy with ghee, poured in oblation upon it to bring safety and prosperity to the city it guards. It is a day of festival, and the city is gay with flags, some presented by the kings to commemorate brave deeds, flying over the homes of captains, and others waving over the shops who sell the gladdening toddy. The streets are broad rivers of people, folk of every race, buying and selling in the marketplace or singing to the music of wandering minstrels.

> Morning comes in the sound of brahmins intoning the Vedas. The wandering bards renew their singing, and the shopkeepers busy themselves opening their booths.

I visited yesterday the room where Ramana Maharshi had his death experience at the age of sixteen:

> I held my breath and kept my lips tightly closed so that no sound could escape, so that neither the word "I" nor any other word could be uttered; "Well then," I said to myself, "this body is dead. It will be carried stiff to the burning ground and there burnt and reduced to ashes. But with the death of this body, am I dead? Am I the body? It is silent and inert but I feel the full force of my personality and even the voice of the "I" within me, apart from it. So I am spirit transcending the body; the body dies but the spirit that transcends it cannot be touched by death. That means I am the deathless spirit.

2

SANKARA Shastri's house is the last one in what was once an *agrahaaram* (brahmin street) near the Vaigai River. He is nearly 90 years old and I study the Shastras under him. He uses magnifying glasses to sift through palm leaves bequeathed by my ancestor, Subbiah, to his great-grandfather. They contain Subbiah's translation of Abhinavagupta's *Tantraloka* in Tamil *grantha* script. In the morning, he gives me a succinct account of the Indian tradition and tells me that in the Vedic Age nobody made a distinction between spiritual life and worldly life, they had an all-comprehensive vision. They communicated with the gods not for their self-realisation but for the welfare of humanity. Shastri tells me, that the *rishi*s prayed that all people may have common thought, common hearing and common intuition in the heart. Shastri tells me about kings who were also self-realised souls and sages of the highest order. "There was King Janaka," he says,

> He was a great ruler and also a great sage. People flocked to his court to get knowledge. He was conversing one day with Yajnavalkya, a great sage, when a messenger came screaming, "Sir, the palace is on fire!" Janaka continued the conversation and did not budge. When the message was repeated, he said: *mithilyam pradiptayam name kinchana dahyati*: Even if the whole Mithila were to be burnt nothing of me would be singed. Such was his detachment. In those days *dharma* was greater than the king and kings had to respect the *dharma* or what is called as *rita* in the Vedas.

Shastri's son brings coffee and we gulp it. I return home after giving my *pranams* to my *guru*. The next day Shastri tells me about five negative prohibitions (*yama*) and five positive injunctions (*niyama*) in Patanjali's *Yoga-Sutra*. They are *ahimsa* (non-violence), *asteya* (non-stealing), *brahmacharya* (celibacy), truth (*satya*), not accepting gifts indiscriminately (*aparigraha*), *tapasya* (purposeful accumulation of energies) and *svadhyaya* (study). Shastri tells me about a saint who was asked who his *guru* was. He replied, "The wind, the sun, the rain, the trees, the animals, the birds, I get lessons from every one of them; they are all my *gurus*." "We have to receive wisdom from wherever it is available," Shastri says, "Finally, *Ishvara-pranidhana*, adoration of the Lord is required. Realisation of divine consciousness is the aim of *yoga*. *Yoga* simply means union with God." Shastri is capable of some rare insights and once he said, "Ours is a special country in the sense that we worship God as Beauty, as Delight, Shyama Sundara. We are not afraid of Him, we love Him. You can see the hand of God everywhere." He finishes the day's lesson with this gem.

3

"INDIA is most Indian in Tamil Nadu where Shiva reigns supreme," Professor K. Swaminathan told me in Chennai. He said "The Tamils have evolved the six-faced God, the rising sun, un-ageing youth — Muruga. For the Tamils, the human dharma of *anbu* (affection) and the felt experience of *inbu* (happiness) are the outer and inner side of every moment truly lived. This God moulds the future with the power of *prema*." According to Kavya Kantha Ganapati Muni, Ramana Maharshi is the modern *avatara* of Muruga:

> The thief who stole the hunter's daughter
> unborn, immortal Muruga
> says, "Be speechless, still," and I
> am pure awareness, being all
> and knowing nothing.

"To remain Indian," the professor continued, "is to see and handle *vyavahara* in the light of *paramartha*, to accept one's given time, place and circumstance and play one's various roles in the world-drama, while remembering one's true being is in the one Awareness — Bliss."

And then the Professor told me about my ancestor Subbiah who was a renowned Advaitic saint, known as Sri Krishna Chaitanya. The Professor directed me to go to Madurai, the Kashi of the South, to study the teaching of Acharya Sankara, Ramana Maharshi and also the life of my ancestor, Subbiah under Sankara Shastri. Shastri has done research on Subbiah's *guru*, a fascinating advaitin saint, Paramahamsa Shivahari who initiated Subbiah into Advaita.

In Madurai, showing me age-old manuscripts, Shastri says,

Shivahari's ancestor Agnihotri migrated from Kannauj in CE 1194 to escape religious persecution by Muslim rulers. Shivahari studied Advaita under his *guru* Vajpeyi in the Narmada Valley. Until the middle of the nineteenth century only a few traditional pandits in Kashmir had access to the philosophy. In 1876, Dr G. Buhler published the entire corpus of *Pratyabhijna* literature and brought it to the notice of the world. His *guru* who had lived in Kashmir gained the knowledge from *pandits* there and passed them on to his disciple, Shivahari.

I also learn that a scholar from Madurai, Madhuraja, in the eleventh century travelled to Kashmir in order to become the disciple of Acharya Abhinavagupta. Madhuraja was then 74 years old and stayed in Kashmir for a little more than a decade. He considered Abhinavagupta as the incarnation of Dakshinamurty. He also wrote a poetic tribute to his *guru*, *Gurunatha Paramarsha*, which is widely quoted by Kashmiri scholars. Swami Lakshman Joo when he came to meet Ramana Maharshi in 1938, mentioned the visit of Madhuraja to Kashmir and said that he was reviving the spiritual link between Madurai and Kashmir.

My wife, Lakshmi, died ten years ago. She had suffered from cancer. I think of her often, but then it seems a long time ago since she died. Sometimes I feel that it is good that she left since she never came out of the shock of the death of Divya in America. Divya was the rebel in the family. She was our only child and we gave her a lot of love and freedom. Lakshmi was from Mumbai and could not adjust to conservative Chennai or Madras as it was called then. "It is too conservative. People are too narrow-minded," she said. I told her, "Chennai is too modern for me. As a professor of English I am forced to live here. Given to myself I would go to my village, Harikesanallur, and live there." "You and your Harikesanallur. You are a typical country chap," she said. But such quarrels were not frequent as I was too busy in my job. Divya grew up in a different environment. As a teenager she frequented parties and returned home late. Lakshmi was also busy in her socialite world. After her graduation, Divya applied to a Research Institute in Delhi. I was praying that she would not get it, but she did well at the entrance examination and joined a course there. "Be a good girl there, dear," I said. "Appa, you are too conservative. One must go along with the times," she said. She was indeed swept away by the times and what times these are! Crass materialism has creeped into every inch of the society. India, which led the world in realms of the spirit, has also fallen prey to this consumerist, soul-denying, narcissist philosophy. The gap between Divya and me widened, though I thought it was only temporary.

Sometimes my mind becomes a battlefield. Memories of clashes with Divya haunt me and I get terribly disturbed. Divya has left the biggest wound and Lakshmi pampered her a lot, ignoring the early signs of moral degeneration.

"The teacher has again complained about Divya. She has beaten up someone in school," I said.

"She is too young, I am sure she is a good girl," Lakshmi said.

Years later, when Divya went to Delhi, she took to smoking and drinking. She told me about her plans of studying in America. She went to America and we hardly heard from her except for an occasional phone call.

"Dad I am alright. Don't be anxious about me," she said over the phone.

"But you don't sound healthy dear," I said. "Give the phone to me and I will talk to her," Lakshmi said, "Divya, What is this? No news from you?"

We received the news after a fortnight that Divya was killed by her boyfriend over a friendly fight in a pub while both were in a heavily inebriated state. He confessed his crime and was arrested. The body arrived in a coffin and both of us were in a state of shock for months. Then everything in my life was like a dream. Lakshmi's death due to cancer, my retirement. . . .

Our ancestors divided life into four *ashramas*, *brahmacharya*, *grihastha*, *vanaprastha* and *sannyasa*. I have reached the *vanaprastha* stage of my life. Professor Max Müller in one of his books describes this stage beautifully:

> Then followed the third stage after a man had fulfilled all his duties, had performed all necessary sacrifices, and had seen the children of his children. Then and only then came the time when he might retire from his house, give up all that belonged to him, and settle somewhere in forest near, with or without his wife, but still accessible to his relations and chiefly occupied in overcoming all passions by means of ascetic exercises, and withdrawing his affections more and more from all things of this life.
>
> During that third station, that of *vanaprastha* or *Bylobios*, the mind of the hermit became more and more concentrated on that higher philosophy which we call religion, and more particularly on the Vedanta, as contained in the Upanishads, and similar later works. Instead of merely dipping into the waters, the philosophical baptism became then a complete submergence, and entrance into life with *Brahman*, where alone perfect peace and a perfect satisfaction of man's spiritual desires could be found.

4

I FIND solace in Tamil Bhakti poets Appar, Sundarar and Manikkavacakar. I visit one temple after the other, by taxi or bus, admiring the bushy, green countryside; the villagers busy in the harvest and merchants commuting from one place to another. I read accounts of the Shaivite poets who poured out their longing for Shiva. Some even saw Him. I also visit the temples nearby reading the hymns in the now neglected shrines and trying to connect myself with my Cosmic Maker. I try my best to forget the past and the effort is not without success. I have understood from my study of Bhagavan Ramana Maharshi that whatever this body is to do and whatever experiences it is to pass through was already decided when it came into existence. He states that others are not responsible for what happens to us. They are only instruments of what would happen to us some way or other:

> All the activities that the body is to go through are determined when it first comes into existence. It does not rest with you to accept or reject them. The only freedom you have is to turn your mind inward and renounce activities there. Nobody can say why that freedom alone and no other freedom is left to man. That is the Divine scheme.

Elsewhere Bhagavan Ramana states that individual human beings have to suffer their *karma*s for his purpose. God manipulates the fruits of *karma*; He does not add or take away from it. The subconsciousness of man is a warehouse of good and bad *karma*s. *Ishvara* chooses from this warehouse what he sees will best suit the spiritual evaluation at the time of each man whether pleasant or painful; thus there is nothing arbitrary.

Thus it is clear that all our experiences should only be

shadows and the substratum is really the Self. The Divine will works its way and remaining witness to this is the only option that we have. Individuality or the ego or the mind is an illusion and the concept of free will lasts only so long as this imposter called individuality exists. Bhagavan Ramana points out that one only has to enquire who really undergoes this destiny and discover that only the ego is bound by it and the self is only a witness. The ego is non-existent. The body takes birth in order to carry out various activities that have already been decided at the time of conception. The only freedom that man has is not to identify himself with the body. Once the realisation, "I am not the body," sets in, the pleasures and pain which are an integral part of all human activities do not affect us. Happiness, as Ramesh Balsekhar later told me in Mumbai, does not exist in the flow of life, which is full of pleasure and pain, but in our attitude towards life. The Divine will prevails in all circumstances and individuals are subject to that will. As Bhagavan Ramana has pointed out again and again, life is only the movie on the screen. The self is the screen which is not affected by the movie. The screen/self alone is the reality. The movie is real only as long as we identify ourselves with the characters. Once we remain detached from it, we remain spectators. The movie of life goes on, the show is full of death, deceit, jealousy, suspicion, back-stabbing, arrogance, conceit, and so on. But such qualities exist only for the mind, and the mind alone is affected. The *sadgurus*, like Bhagawan Ramana, ask this question, "Does this mind exist in deep sleep?"

5

THE poetry of Muruganaar, that divinely inspired poet who surrendered to Ramana Maharshi, also comes to my rescue:

> I have ended the confusion of my bewildered, suffering mind.
>
> A lowly cur, I have merged with the gracious feet of my Master.
>
> In the surging brilliance of his divine wisdom's splendour the broad ocean of deadly desires has disappeared completely.

I have stopped worrying about this and that, trying to focus my mind on the self. Lakshmi and Divya, the problems I had faced in my office, everything seems to be an illusion, the *maya* of *Brahman*:

> The dark prison which bound my tortured soul crumbled and I became his servant, finding joyous life in the open sky of his ambrosial grace. The knot which locked my spirit to my physical body was sundered by the bright sword of my Master's glance and was no more.

I think about my accomplishments and feel the futility and meaninglessness of human endeavours:

> I was a learned fool. My flawed mind knew nothing till I came to dwell with him whose glance filled my heart with the light of awareness. Dwelling in that gracious state of peace, whose nature is holy silence, so hard to gain and know, I entered into union with the deathless state of the knowledge of reality.
>
> As the deadly delusion of a body-bound ego faded, a flower of pure light unfolded at his holy feet. That radiance grew ever brighter with my lover until I realised the flawless

knowledge of the self, manifesting as the unbroken awareness "I-I" within my heart.

The ego is the basis of all sorrows and it converts us into beasts running after ephemeral pleasures. The story of Tattvaraya who composed a poem in honour of his Guru Svarupananda is interesting. He asked a congregation of *pandit*s to assess the value of the work. The *pandit*s objected to the poem on the ground that poems were only written about great heroes capable of killing a thousand elephants and not about a saint. Tattvaraya said, "Let us all go to my *guru* and we shall settle this matter there." They went to Guru Svarupananda and told him the purpose of their visit. The Guru was silent and the group went into *mauna*. Days and nights passed and yet they sat silently. After four days, the Guru emerged out of his silence and the group also regained its normal activities relating to thought. They immediately declared, "Conquering 1,000 elephants is nothing beside this Guru's power to conquer the elephants of all our egos put together. So certainly he deserves the poem in his honour." Self-enquiry helps us to pierce through the ego and realise our true nature.

Reading through the talks of Bhagavan Ramana, I experience bliss and remain totally detached from my actions annihilating the sense of doership, and remaining fixed in the self. Bhagavan Ramana said, "If one keeps fixed in the self, the activities will still go on and their success will not be affected. One should not have the idea that one is the doer. The activities will still go on. That force, by whatever name you may call it, which brought the body into existence will see to it that the activities which this body is meant to go through are brought about." It was Bhagavan Ramana who taught me to consider only the self as real and regard oneself as an actor who dresses for his part in the drama. Such a person knows fully well that he is not that character but someone else in real life. In the same manner the feeling that "I am not the body but the self" and decimation of body consciousness help to maintain inner bliss. When we abide in the self, we let the body play its role in the cosmic drama like an actor doing his role on the stage. The self is the screen and life is the cinema shown on the screen. Remain fixed on the screen — that was the message of Bhagavan Ramana to me. Life is full of anxieties and the hysteria of everyday life disorients us. Bhagavan Ramana helps us to negotiate our way through pleasure and pain, hope and anxiety, and discover inner happiness which is our real nature. My study of the life of Subbiah and Paramahamsa Shivahari along with Vedantic studies with Sankara Shastri helps me to reconstruct the broken edifice of my life. Ganapati Shastri, Subbiah's father, had a brother called Neelakanta Shastri and I am his great-grandson. With the help of manuscripts left behind by Subbiah I re-live the 1860s when life was totally different. I dream about their journey from place to place in search of eternal truth.

6

I ASK Sankara Shastri, "Why this loss of *dharma*, divorces, suicides, etc.? Why has India become like this?"

He replies, "The Paramacharya of Kanchi rightly pointed out that we brahmins are responsible for the decline of Hinduism. We gave up the duties of our birth — the study of the Vedas. We migrated from villages to the towns. We took up the learning of the West. We dumped the Shastras and took up Western living. The Shastras declare emphatically that the brahmin must have no love for money and not accumulate wealth. So long as we studied the Vedas and lived the Vedic life, the entire society respected us. They knew that the brahmin chanted the Vedas solely for the welfare of the society. Later, when we gave up our traditional life and started making money, other communities too gave up their traditional occupation. For thousands of years, the brahmin dedicated his life to the study of the *atman*. He used his intellect only for the benefit of society. Now he is only interested in his own advancement. As the Paramacharya said, due to sheer momentum the bicycle keeps going some distance even after you stop pedalling. The success of the brahmin in the secular and scientific world in the last hundred years is solely due to the "pedalling" done by his forefathers. The brahmin, who did not give up his Vedic duties even during Islamic rule, was enamoured of the new sciences during British rule most of which was meant only to pander to the senses. Following the brahmin all members gave up their traditional occupation, and handicrafts were neglected. Previously there was no confrontation or rivalry among different communities. Each caste studied the Shastra of its occupation. The new system has created jealousy, disputes and hatred.

"Due to the "pedalling" of his ancestors, the brahmin became successful in the secular world. He gave up his *dharma*. The British concocted the Aryan-Dravidian theory and created friction between brahmins and non-brahmins. This hatred towards brahmins emerged only after the British period.

"Since the brahmin competed with others in secular jobs, he became an object of hatred, though he spoke about equality. In earlier times he was highly respected because he studied the Vedas and engaged in spiritual pursuits for the welfare of society. As the Paramacharya said, the brahmin spoiled himself and spoiled others. If in the past he was respected for his austere lifestyle, discipline and spiritual elevation, he came to be hated in the modern age for his moral degeneration. He pursued the sense objects.

"The Shastras declare that the brahmin is not to utilise his body for sense enjoyment. He had to maintain high ideals. The Shastras require him to wake up at four in the morning and bathe in cold water. Then he has to perform one rite after another, *sandhya-vandana, brahmayajna, upasana, puja* and one of the 21 sacrifices. He cannot eat cold rice in the morning. His day time meal will be only at 1 o'clock. His dwelling resembled the hut of a peasant. He had no right to earn or borrow money.

"The Paramacharya quotes from the *Mahabharata* to illustrate the simple life of the brahmin:

> *pancame hani saste va sakam pacatisvegrhe* |
> *anrni ca 'pravasi ca savaricara modate* ||

"If daytime is divided into eight parts, the brahmin may eat his food only in the fifth or sixth part after performing all his rites. Before that he has neither any breakfast nor any snacks. And what does he eat? Not any rich food, no sweets like almonds crushed in sweetened milk. *Sakam pacati* the brahmin eats leafy vegetables growing on the banks of rivers, such areas being no one's property. Why is he asked to live by the riverside? It is for his frequent baths and for the leafy vegetables, growing trees there and for which he does not have to beg. He should not borrow money; that is the meaning of the word *anrni,* because if he developed the habit of borrowing he would be tempted to lead a life of luxury. Poverty and non-acquisitiveness (*aparigraha*) are his ideals. A brahmin ought not to keep even a blade of grass in excess of his needs. *Apravasam* means that a brahmin must not leave his birthplace and settle elsewhere."

Sankara Shastri opens a page from a book titled *Hindu Dharma* written by the Paramacharya and quotes from a passage,

"It is alleged that brahmins created the Dharmashastras for their own benefit. You will realise that this charge is utterly baseless if you appreciate the fact that these Shastras impose on them the most stringent rules of life. There is also proof of the impartiality of the Dharmashastras in that the brahmin who is expected to be proficient in all the arts and all branches of learning can only give instruction in them but cannot take up any for his livelihood however lucrative it be and however less demanding than the pursuit of the Vedic Dharma.

"Now it is claimed that all people are equal in all spheres, that all are equal before the law. But members of the legislative bodies, judges, etc. enjoy certain privileges and cannot be treated on the same footing as the common man. People who call themselves democrats and socialists have managed for themselves special allowances, special railway passes, etc. that the common people are not entitled to. In contrast, the brahmins who preserved the Dharmashastras bound themselves to vigorous discipline, roasted themselves, as it were, in the oven of ritual practices."

"You have given me plenty of ideas, Shastri," I say and take leave of him.

"Could you please tell me about the greatest achievement of Acharya Sankara?," I ask him the next day. Sankara Shastri takes a glass of water from an earthern jar and says, "Sundar, one of Acharya Sankara's greatest achievements is his commentary on the *Gita*. Sankara's introduction to his *Gita Bhashya* is equally famous. Firstly the Acharya quotes a Puranic verse:

> *narayanah paro avyaktat andamavyakta sambhavam* ।
> *andasyantastvime lokah saptadvipa ca medini* ।।

Narayana (the Supreme Divine Being) is beyond the *avyakta* (undifferentiated Nature); the Cosmic Egg has come out of the *avyakta*; within the cosmic egg are these universes including the earth with its seven island continents.

Nature has two dimensions — *avyakta* (the undifferentiated state) and *vyakta* (differentiated). From *avyakta* comes the *vyakta*, the manifested, the *brahmanda* (the cosmic egg). The whole *brahmanda* has come from *Brahman*, and gets dissolved into *Brahman* at the end of a cosmic cycle.

The *dharma* of the Vedas is twofold containing *pravritti* (outward action) and *nivritti* (inward contemplation) which are meant to ensure *abhyudaya* (socio-economic welfare) and *nihshreyasa* (spiritual freedom) of everyone. An integrated person should combine *pravritti* and *nivritti*. Meditate and go deeper inside yourself. Realise that you are not the body, mind or the intellect. Come in contact with the self.

This twofold *dharma* was practised for long ages by all sections of people, desirous of spiritual welfare, like brahmins and members of other three *varna*s and members of the four *ashrama*s.

Those who practised this *dharma* due to lack of discrimination and wisdom developed excessive sensory desires, with the

> result that *dharma* or value awareness was overthrown and *adharma* or social evils multiplied.

Shastri placed the book aside and said,

> When man is overcome by *kama* and *krodha* (lust and anger) he becomes bereft of *viveka* (capacity for discrimination) and *vijnana* (wisdom). *Dharma* decreases and *adharma* increases.

He again read a verse from the book:

> Therefore, with a view to ensuring the well-being of the world, the primal-world projecting, that Lord celebrated as Vishnu, known as Narayana was born of Vasudeva (father) through Devaki's (mother) as Krishna, in order to protect the brahmanhood of the earth.

Here brahmanhood does not refer to any caste. It essentially is about knowledge of the *Brahman*. So it is important for us to understand the perennial philosophy of the *Bhagavad-Gita*.

7

I GO to my room and open a biography of Sri Sankara I purchased in Chennai. I also revise the notes on the classes on Vedanta by Sankara Shastri. It gives me immense pleasure to connect myself with the higher force. Sankara Shastri has taught me that *Brahman* is the primordial cause of the universe. *Brahman* is *satyam* (truth), *jnanam* (knowledge) *anantam* (limitless). The world is nothing but *Brahman*. In spite of the different appearances, water, ice and steam are H_2O only. The ignorant is deceived by the false appearance and sees the world as different from *Brahman*. The Vedas are *apaurusheya,* not man-made. They have a musical structure. They are vast. There are no contradictions in the Vedas and they contain a lot of scientific truth. The *Brihadaranyaka Upanishad* states, "The soul lives in the right eye and so he is called Dakshinakshipurusha. He rules all the worlds and the desires in man." These *mantra*s are discussed in the *Brahma-Sutras* as well. Scientists now say that the left part of the human brain handles a person's speech, the time analysis of events and calculations. The right side is responsible for the study of time and space and the handling of ideas.

Coming to the question of what evolved first, the seed or the tree? Botanists now say that it was the tree that evolved first. Tissue culture has also developed. The *Chhandogya Upanishad* states, "it is only the tree which is the seed of the tree so also the bird is the seed of the bird and not the egg." This means that in creation it was only the tree that appeared first. Sri Sankara states on this *shloka,* "When we are observing that it is the seed which is the seed of the tree, how can the Vedas say that the tree is the seed of the tree?" Then he says,

"Yes, If the Vedas depended on your intelligence, it could not have made that statement. But remember that the Vedas are an independent source of knowledge. Moreover, don't we see that many plants are born without seeds though no seed is born without a plant? Therefore we cannot doubt the Vedic statement."

I continue my studies of the Shastras and each day gives me renewed energy. My reading of translations of the *Ramayana* and the *Mahabharata* makes me admire the intellectual and sprititual depth of India. The *rishis*, as Sri Aurobindo wrote, recognised the distinction between *karana* and *pratishtha*, the North Pole and South Pole of being. The Earth or gross matter is the *pratishtha*, *Brahman* or spirit is the *karana*. Raising our level of consciousness and lifting ourselves from the base animal level to the spiritual is *brahmacharya*. In the modern world we are carried away by the objects of pleasure and neglect the divine in us. Pampering our animal-like body and enslaved by our senses, we have created a miserable world, miserable for us and for others. It is high time we reflected on the real meaning of India.

Acharya Sankara said, "The magician is real, the magic is unreal. In the same way *Brahman* is real, the world is unreal." Ramakrishna Paramahamsa said, the magician performs his magic. He produces a mango tree which even bears mangoes. But this is all sleight of hand. The magician alone is real. The *Mahanirvana Tantra* says "*mayaya kalpitam jagat*, The visible world is a projection of *maya*. Nothing exists without *Brahman*."

The *Katha Upanishad* says that, "our sense organs are by nature outgoing. The Lord made them that way. That is why we are not able to see the self within. We perceive only the outer object. But a calm person, desiring immortality, beholds the inner self with his eyes closed." Ramakrishna asked his devotees to "give up the unripe "I" which makes one feel: "I am the doer." Renounce this "unripe I" and keep the "ripe I" which will make you feel that you are the servant of God, His devotee and God is the doer and you are His instrument."

8

SANKARA Shastri takes the *Gospel of Sri Ramakrishna* and reads from it: "The Intervention of this ego creates the difference between the *jiva* and *atman*. Water appears to be divided into two parts if one puts a stick across it. But in reality there is only one water. It appears as two on account of the stick. This "I" is the stick. Remove the stick and there remains only one water as before. "Thinking 'I am the doer' is ignorance. But O Lord, thou art the driver and I am the machine. This is knowledge. If by the grace of God, a man but once realises that he is not the doer, then at once he becomes a *jivanmukta*. Though living in the body, he is liberated. Smear your hands with oil before opening the jackfruit (that is, be immersed in the self while involving yourself in worldly matters). Be like the mother turtle that swims in the water but has her mind on the banks of the river where the eggs are."

Sankara Shastri continues, Sri Krishna says to Arjuna:

sarvadharman parityajya mamekan sharanam vraja I
aham tvam sarvapapebhyo mokshayishyemi ma sucah II

Abandoning all duties, come to me alone for shelter.
Be not grieved, for I shall release thee from all evils.

Or as the Upanishads say:

sarvajive sarvasamsthe brihante
asmin hamso bhramyate brahmacakre
prithagatmanam preritaram camatra
justastataste namritatvameti

In the great wheel of *Brahman* in which all things abide and finally take rest, the *jiva* wanders about so long as it thinks that it is separate from the controller. When blessed by Him, the self attains immortality.

Acharya Sankara says in *Atmabodha*:

tirtva moharnavam hatva
ragadveshadirakshasan
yogi santisamayukta
atmaramo virajate

Having crossed the ocean of delusion and having killed the monsters of attachment and aversion the *yogi* becomes united with peace and dwells in the Bliss derived from the realisation of the self alone.

Again the Acharya says:

bahyanitya sukhasatim
hitvatmasukhanirvritah
ghatasthadipavatsvasthah
svantareva prakashate

Relinquishing attachment to illusory external happiness, the self-abiding *jivanmukta,* satisfied with the bliss derived from the *atman,* shines inwardly like a lamp placed inside a jar.

The *Shvetashvatara Upanishad* says:

eko devah sarvabhuteshu gudhah
sarvavyapi sarvabhutantaratma

The non-dual and resplendent lord is hidden in all beings. All-pervading. He is the innermost self of all creatures.

I return to my room immersed in the verses of Sri Sankara. The philosophy of non-dualism helps me to reconcile myself to the strange nature of the human condition. Sankara has given me strength. Yet the residue of *vasana*s remains. My *sadhana* is progressing and back in my room I keep reflecting on the self. My mind has accumulated a lot of desires and resentments over the years and these toxins kill my system, destroying harmony and equilibrium of thought and action. As Sankara Shastri tells me, the mind is the cause of both bondage and liberation, *mana eva manushyanam karanam bandha mokshayoh*. Control of mind, thought, speech, action, desire (*kama*) and anger (*krodha*) is essential. Fear and sorrow keep haunting us, weakening our system and bringing negative vibrations:

> *saknoteehaiva yassodhum prak sharira vimoksha nat* |
> *kama-krodhodbhavam vegam sa yuktah sasukhi narah* ||

> After death a man is what he has been just before his death. If he has not controlled lust and anger in this life, and acquired peace of mind and joy, he cannot have them after death.

Sri Sankara keeps repeating, *ihaiva* meaning here itself. Liberation is possible in this life itself. No other religion promises heavenly happiness here, on earth itself. It is the happiness of a man who has shed his ego and is immersed in the self. There is no need to aspire for joy in heaven, when it is there right within us.

Sankara Shastri's house "Tapovan" is full of manuscripts of the epics and the Shastras. Shastri pores over the *Brahma-Sutra* late into the night, gets up at four in the morning, goes to the Vaigai and takes his bath, does his *sandhya*. He is assisted by his son, Kannan, who works as a priest in a temple. Shastri is trying to bring out a revised, annotated edition of the *Brahma-Sutra*, as he is dissatisfied with the available editions in Sanskrit. He strictly follows the *Bhashya* of Sankara in his preparation of the *Brahma-Sutra* edition and hopes that some publisher would evince interest in it. "Who is interested in such things in this *Kaliyuga*?" he often says, "But still I will not give up hope." "Don't worry, Acharya, the Lord himself will help a noble soul like you," I tell him. "Yes, In *atma-vidya* we must not be cynical," he says.

He continues his lessons, "*Brahman* is the only reality. *Brahman* is one, but appears to us as many on the relative plane. The potter knows that all objects made of clay appear as different in name and form but are from the same substance. When you remove name and form from a jar you get only earth. Due to ignorance the phenomenal world is projected to us. It is the *maya* of *Brahman*. The *atman* is the illuminator of everything. Through a *guru*, when you see the essence which is its substratum, then you will abide in the self, as Ramana Maharshi said. We mistake the serpent for the rope due to this ignorance. A realised soul sees *Brahman* alone. He sees the rope and not the snake. Through the *guru* you will be able to realise the truth of the rope or *Brahman* and the delusion of snake or creation will vanish. *Brahman* should be realised like an *amla* fruit in one's hand. Then the worshipper and the worshipped, the meditator and the object of meditation, the knower and the known, all become one. We realise that everything is *Brahman* or the self."

"What about *Ishvara*?" I ask.

"The Supreme Reality is not a person. The *jiva* is an individual and the sum total of all *jiva*s is the *Ishvara*. *Avidya* dominates the *jiva*. *Ishvara* projects this world out of Himself and He controls *maya*, consisting of *avidya* and *vidya*. *Brahman* is beyond the *jiva* and *Ishvara*. There are no modifications on *Brahman* and the *jiva* and the Universe are superimposed on *Brahman*. The universe consists only in name and form. The goal of Advaita is to realise that I am *Brahman*. Ignoring this true identity the *jiva* goes through the cycle of births and deaths. Remember, this body is only an instrument. The *purusha* within is your real nature. Go beyond the five sheaths (matter, breath, mind, intellect, bliss) that *bind* you and know that you are the eternal *atman*. Meditate that I am not this body, mind, intellect. Kill the mind. The knower, known, meditator and the object meditated upon become one. All phenomenal superimpositions will disappear. He who knows the *Brahman* becomes *Brahman*."

"And what about birth, death and creation?," I ask

"So long as you identify yourself with your body, and possess ego, such things remain. When you get rid of them and live in the *atman* such questions will disappear"

"And the Divine Mother?"

"Shakti is the acting power of *Brahman*. It is *Brahman* in manifestation. Ramakrishna Paramahamsa illustrated it with the example of 'snake moving and snake at rest'."

"Acharya, please help me to gain self-knowledge."

"Ramana Maharshi has recommended the technique of self-enquiry. He asked the famous question, Who am I? The *Kena Upanishad* begins with the question, "Who is it that enables the mind to think, the *prana* to function, the ears to hear, the eyes to see?" Discriminate between the "seer" and the "seen." The self is a witness to the movements of the senses and the mind. Consciousness is the cause of all human activities. The self is the innermost light of consciousness, showing us the Kutastha Chaitanya. The sage Vamadeva, in the *Brihadaranyaka Upanishad*, while realising this (self) as *Brahman*, said, "I was Manu, and the sun." This "I" is the self and not the waking "I" or dreaming "I." In *Shvetashvatara Upanishad*, the sage says:

> Hear O ye children of immortality, even gods and angels, I have discovered my true self, that ancient infinite being within my heart, that light of all lights beyond all darkness. By finding him, one can conquer death. There is no other way.

"The body of a devotee, as Sri Ramakrishna said, is the playground of consciousness. Heaven descends on the body which practises *japa* with faith. The *Kena Upanishad* says, one who realises the existence of *Brahman* behind every activity whether sensation, perception or thought, that person alone gains immortality. The *Chhandogya Upanishad* describes a dialogue between Narada and Sanatkumara. Narada wanted to gain knowledge from Sanatkumara. Sanatkumara asked, "Please tell me what you know; afterwards I shall tell you what is beyond." Narada replied: "I know the *Rigveda*, the *Yajurveda*, the *Samaveda*, the *Atharvaveda*, history and mythology, grammar, the rules for the sacrifices for the ancestors, the science of numbers, logic." Narada knew almost everything. "All these are only names," said Sanatkumara. "All this knowledge is nothing. That is why you have no peace." Narada said, "Yes, these are only words. This is only a list of the branches of knowledge that I have studied. I have heard from other people that a person who knows the self crosses over sorrow. What is this self? I am in a state of grief in spite of all this learning. I have come to you, great master, with a request to take me beyond the ocean of sorrow. I do not know the real substance of all these arts and sciences. The name is known, but the content is not known to me. I have heard that if one knows the self of a thing, he would be free from sorrow." Sanatkumara gave *Brahma-vidya* to Narada taking the saint into the forest of Vedanta in which the Kohinoor of *atman* is located. Ultimately everything boils down to the question, who am I? What is this "I"? Is it the individual "I" or the ego? Is it the body, the mind or the intellect? No, it is the *atman* which says, "I am here, I am there and everywhere." The space within the vessel is identical with the space in the universe outside. There is no distinction between a pot space or space in a tumbler and the space outside. The distinctions that we create are imaginary. There is no inner space and outer space. The universe is *atman* in all things. It is the essential subject of everything. So, that which is cosmically present as the total object is also the total subject. In a universal sense it is the subject and object.

"One who has attained this realisation is the happiest person conceivable. Such a person is delighted within his own self, he plays with his own self, and he enjoys his own self, in short such a person is rooted in the bliss of his own self. This self is the universal being, *Brahman* pervading everywhere. A person with this realisation becomes a master of himself and has mastery of all things. He attains self-mastery over the universe. He becomes self-emperor, self-king, ruling over the self. Such a person rules over everything everywhere. Self-kingship, *atma svarajya* leads to universal lordship. People with this knowledge get cosmic freedom. They can enter into every plane of existence. People without this knowledge are controlled by other people and lead a limited life. They take one birth after another due to this ignorance. If you imagine that there are things outside one's self, you become controlled by those things outside you. If you lead an external life, those externals will subjugate you. Such people only get sorrow in life. They remain *jiva*s and never realise that they are really the *atman*. That is what we see everywhere. People, without even realising the divinity within them, trying to get happiness by hurting others, dominating, bullying, slander-mongering. Our Shastras say that this is the nature of beasts."

9

I DISCOVER my grandfather's daily routine, after retirement from government service, from an old diary maintained by him. Here it is:

3.00 a.m.	Short prayer at the time of rising, ablutions and bath.
4.15 a.m.	*Puja*. (He had his own *puja* articles; during *puja* he recited the *Gita*.)
5.00 a.m.	*Surya namaskara* (yogic exercise).
6.00 a.m.	Walk for an hour. He recited the *Gita* while walking.
7.00 a.m.	Milk.
7.30 a.m.	Reading *Valmiki*.
10.30 a.m.	Morning meal: cow's milk, fruits (one apple and bananas) rest for an hour after lunch, just lying down, not sleeping.
1.00 p.m.	*Gayatri* for one hour.
2.30 p.m.	*Valmiki* again.
5.00 p.m.	Evening walk for 30 to 40 minutes.
6.00 p.m.	Evening meal: milk and fruits.
	(He followed strictly the rules of the Shastras which do not permit us to eat in hotels or outside.)
6.45 p.m.	*Sandhya* prayers.
9.00 p.m.	Short prayer before going to bed.

He read *Yoga-Vasistha* and *Narada-Bhakti-Sutras* frequently. This enabled him to maintain equanimity under all circumstances. He religiously adhered to the *Gita*'s definition of a brahmin:

> Restraint (of mind), restraint of senses, penance, cleanliness, endurance, guilelessness, knowledge, realisation, faith in the scriptures — these constitute the work of Brahmins.

Such discipline and spiritual vigilance enabled him to lead a harmonious life, alas! that is now broken in our world.

10

KUMARILA Bhatta was a true brahmin. A champion of Purva-Mimamsa, he had studied the Shastras in the *gurukula*. Later he studied under a Buddhist *guru*, disguised as a monk. When his *guru* discovered his true identity and Bhatta's attachment to the Vedas, he conspired to throw Kumarila from the terrace. "If the Vedas are true nothing will happen to me," Kumarila thought and though he was hurled from the top, he survived. He became an opponent of Buddhism. "I have committed the sin of *guru-dosha*," Kumarila thought, as he had lied to his *guru* about his interest in Buddhism. "I will burn myself in the *tusanala* (burning chaff) as a *prayaschitta* (repentance). When Sankara came to meet him, he had already entered the funeral pyre. He asked Sankara to meet Mandana Misra for a debate on Mimamsa. "Please chant the *Taraka mantra* for my peaceful end," he requested Sankara and saw his body consumed by fire under the echoes of Sankara's chanting.

This is brahmanatva! Giving up the body for violating the Shastras! Writing these lines at 4 a.m. in the morning, the *brahma-muhurtta*, I get visions of Dakshinamurty, the *guru*, while chanting the *shloka*s taught by Sankara Shastri. These verses link me to the life blood of my ancestor, Subbiah and in getting the spirit of brahminhood.

11

I HAVE an appointment today with a *sannyasi* who was formerly a professor in the university. He also taught in a university in the West for a brief period, before embracing asceticism. He studied Vedanta, especially Sankara's *Bhashyas*. I meet him in his apartment. He is in his ochre robes and has piercing eyes. Offering me coffee, he says:

"The Vedas are *apaurusheya*. They explain the *atman* and *Brahman* and conclude that both are same. *Brahman* is *brihat* (limitless), from which everything is born and which expands itself into the work. Everything is *Brahman*. *Shruti* says that one who knows not the Vedas knows not *Brahman*. *Brahman* is revealed through the Upanishads. The aim of the study of the Upanishads is *moksha* (liberation). The *Brahma-Sutra*, composed by sage Badarayana, clears ambiguity, regarding the Shruti, created by the emergence of different philosophical schools. The first chapter Jijnasa-adhyaya establishes that the *Brahman* is to be known. The second chapter, Samanvaya-Adhyaya states that all Vedanta *vakyas* lead to the knowledge of one and the same *Brahman*. The third chapter Avirodha-adhyaya clarifies the errors in schools of thought other than Vedanta. The fourth chapter, Sadhana-adhyaya deals with the methods of attaining *Brahman*.

"The *sutras* are pregnant with meaning, but difficult to understand. Sankaracharya's *Bhashya* has explained the work clearly. In the *Bhashya* he introduces his theory of *adhyasa* (superimposition). Ignorance has to be removed to gain knowledge. Acharya Sankara states that the self is the ultimate reality. The Self or *Brahman* has no qualities in the ordinary sense and is of the nature of pure being, pure consciousness and pure bliss. *Brahman* is the material cause of the world. Creation is due to the *maya* of *Brahman*. From the viewpoint of *maya*, *Brahman* can be conceived of as a personal God."

"What about cause and effect?," I ask.

"Is there difference between moulded pot and clay? There is no difference between cause and effect. The world as caused by *Brahman* is an illusory superimposition (*adhyasa*) of phenomenon on the Supreme Reality. A rope is mistaken for a snake," he observes.

"I am still confused about the self," I say.

"Each of us exists as separate individuals. We say, "I achieved," "I won," "I saw." What is "I"? "Is it my body, mind, intellect, soul, etc.? Where do "I" go when "I" am asleep? The word "I" can have four different meanings:

(a) The knower or inner consciousness
(b) The *antahkarana*
(c) The ego
(d) The *jiva* or Soul

"The *antahkarana* is the material, thinking and perceiving mind. Sankara wants us to use this thorn to extract the thorn of *avidya* (nescience) and realise the self. The self cannot be described. The Upanishads recommend the *neti, neti* (not this! not this!) method of discovering the self. The self is not the ego, which is a physical thing with attributes. We say, "I was arrogant 10 years ago, I was jealous when she published the book," etc. Definitely to make such statements, there must be a "knower" who is a witness to the ego. The self is the witness and it is different from the body and mind. The *antahkarana* mistakes the soul or *jiva* to be the self. The self is different from the *jiva*. The individual self shares the same relationship with the pure self (*Brahman*) as the space within a pot is connected to universal space. The words *atman* and *Brahman* or the individual self and the universal self are employed synonymously by both the Upanishads and Sankara. *Brahman* is the transcendental aspect of the self (in worldly terms, the creator) and *atman* is the individual aspect. To the *jnani Brahman* is the sole reality and what we see in the world are only the ways of *prakriti* consisting of the three *gunas* — sattvic, rajasic and tamasic. *Ishvara* is fond of the individual who asks for self-realisation and not caught in the *maya* of *prakriti*."

12

THE *guru-shishya* relationship is a miraculous relationship. The *guru* is a miracle; the disciple is also a miracle. The *Bhagavad-Gita* says that it is a miracle. All great things in the world are wonders. Swami Sivananda used to say that the whole of *yoga* is self-restraint and simultaneous self-recovery. "It is dying to live," he said. The process of *vairagya* and *abhyasa* constitutes a sort of dying, for the sake of living in a higher sense. He said that a rising of the spirit from this world involvement is not a loss of contact or relationship with the world, it is a rising to the consciousness of the true nature of things. He said that the urge of the finite in the direction of the infinite is a perennial call from the infinite. It is an incessant movement of the finite towards the infinite — like the movement of waters in a river.

Sankara Shastri says, "The philosophy of India may be summed up by the word *yajna,* sacrifice. Every moment of our life is a sacrifice that we perform for a higher fulfilment. *Yajna* means bring the higher power into one's own self, the surrender of the lower self to the superior self. In fact, such words are used in order to help the spiritual aspirant raise himself spiritually. We are connected with everything in the world, with everything in creation. We should not assert our individuality as though we have no connection with the world. There are various types of selfishness, for instance attachment to one's own body. Egoism makes some people bully others and psychologically themselves over others.

"The *yajna* in the *Bhagavad-Gita* helps us to overcome these and tune ourselves to the larger self. We are connected with other people and to the *tanmatra*s (five elements: earth, water, fire, air, ether). Our body is a sophisticated apparatus containing the sense organs, the *pranas*, the mind and the intellect. Self-control requires you to understand that the perceptions of the senses are wrong. They brainwash us. We inhabit a sense world. It conditions our thinking process and the intellect. So self-control means mind-control, intellect-control, reason-control. Sivananda said that the control of one's self is the essence of *yoga*. Self-restraint and self-control lead us to restraint of consciousness. The thought process leads to joys and sorrows. Our mind is the individualised consciousness. The activity of consciousness is inseparable from our ego, the intellect, the reason. Self-control helps it to settle in its own self. Patanjali says, "The restraint of the mind is *yoga*, and then there is establishment of self in its own self" (*yogah chitta vritti nirodhah; tada drashtuh svarupe avasthanam*). Every perception involves a degree of loss of self-consciousness. When we love a thing or hate a thing, part of our personality moves towards that. That weakens us. One who likes or hates is a weak person. Bring the mind back to its centre. Strengthen the mind for higher concentration. We waste precious energy always conscious of somebody else. This involvement in "otherness" has put us in this miserable condition. We worry over what is not there and ignore what is there.

"*Yajna* is inner training. The *Bhagavad-Gita* states:

> The means of the sacrificial offering is *Brahman*; *Brahman* is the oblation placed in the fire of *Brahman* and by *Brahman* is the sacrifice made. This sacrificer, who concentrates on the act that is *Brahman*, reaches *Brahman* alone.

Plunge inward and gain knowledge of one's own self. Once you realise the meaning of the *mahavakya* "*tattvamasi* — you are that" — and understand that the *atman* or your own self is *Brahman*, then all doubts, sorrows will disappear. The *Gita* states:

> Elevate the self by the self; do not weaken the self. Self is indeed the friend of the self. Self alone is self's foe.

"All Western literature deals with the personality, individuality. In our system, this "I-consciousness" is a phenomenal appearance."

"Swami, I read somewhere that our last thought before death decides the future," I observe.

"Yes, but the last thought is the culmination of the total psychological operations of an individual throughout one's life. The last thought is not an isolated one. It is the logical development. We reap what we sow. All the impulses in our life will determine the last thought. Pray to God. Everything will be fine. There is nothing outside God, external to God or superior to God. God is the indwelling self in everyone. God is the supreme parent. His love emanates everywhere. God is never unkind or unjust. God provides us with everything. The Lord says in the *Gita*, "Wherever there is exaltation of any kind, power, knowledge, capacity, it is a supernormal manifestation of anything in this world, it may be artistic capacity, literature, music, administration, whatever it can be, where there is a supernormal expression of this characteristic or endowment, know thou, I am present and in these it is the glory of God, seen by God only. He sees Himself. He loves Himself. Man in his delusion considers himself to be the master of the world.

"There was a brahmin who adored the *Bhagavad-Gita*. He was extremely poor, begging for his food everyday. Yet he had total confidence in the Almighty. Finally no food was available and his family starved. But he kept repeating the verse from the *Gita* — *ananyas chintayanto mam ye janah paryupasate; tesham nityabhiyuktanam yogakshemam vahamyaham* (If you resort to Me, it shall be My duty to take care of you. I shall provide you with all your requirements, and I shall also see that what you have been provided with is secure). Though he was very poor, he said, "God will provide me with what I want. I need not worry." His family starved for three days and his old mother said. "That verse is false. Throw out the *Bhagavad-Gita*." The brahmin struck that verse, in the palm leaf, with a nail, tore it and threw it away. He walked through the streets, very frustrated. A boy, with his tongue bleeding, came running to the house with a bag of rice and rations. "My master, the father of the home, has sent this," he said and started to leave. "Thank you," the mother said, "But why are you bleeding?" "Oh," the boy said. "Your man was very angry for my delay in bringing you this that he tore my tongue." He left. When the brahmin returned he was informed about this. He wept and said, "I never sent any boy. It was Lord Krishna himself, God is never unkind or cruel."

13

THE Upanishadic *rishi*s have revealed to us that heaven is not somewhere above, but within us; in the state of *sahaja* we experience bliss even in the living state. It is a state without thoughts and can be enjoyed by ignorant mortals in deep sleep. Muruganaar said:

> Destroy the false idea of two worlds
> That of earth and that of heaven
> Experience here and now,
> The wholesome truth of oneness,
> Shiva's own auspicious bliss.

Ramana Maharshi's illumination took place in Madurai and Meenakshi guided him to Arunachala. Ramana Maharshi accepted the body's death, like Nachiketas of the *Katha Upanishad*, and understood that man's real nature is the shining self within. I keep looking at the Maharshi's photogenic face and his *brahmastra*, "Who am I?" is my most sacred *mantra*. Shiva is pure awareness, and Madurai is the abode of Shiva and Shakti. The *punyabhumi* Madurai has made me realise that our essential nature is Being-Awareness-Bliss. The state of *Sacchidananda* makes one love everyone. As the *Bhagavad-Gita* tells us, there is no question of loving our neighbour, since we are our neighbour. It was at Cuddalore at a Shiva temple that I got this call first to look within. I had gone to Cuddalore for a marriage and visited the Padaleshwarar Temple and there I got a vision of Shiva instructing me to withdraw from worldly affairs.

In Sanskrit and many Indian languages the word for art is *kala*. *Ka* refers to *Brahman*. The aim of art in the Hindu tradition is to lead us to *Brahman*. I start my biographical work on Paramahamsa Shivahari and Subbiah with this goal in mind.

14

It was 1860. The *agrahaaram* at Harikesanallur had four prominent houses. The poet, Rama Sharma, composed poems in Sanskrit and Tamil. He had a beard and wore spotless clothes. The Bhagavatar, Lakshmanan, did *Harikatha* performances. He was in great demand in the villages in the region for *Harikatha* performances. Subbiah's family was less prosperous. They were a traditional Vaidika (Vedic) family and the only one in the street which maintained the *agnihotra*. Most of the people in the street belonged to the landed gentry and had plenty of leisure. They sat on the pyol and gossiped about zamindars and commoners. Subbiah's family did not own land and they lived in abject poverty. With an umbrella in his hands, his father Ganapati Shastri went to several places since great Sanskrit *pandit*s longed to converse with him about the Dharmashastras. The zamindar also patronised his scholarship. Ganapati Shastri told Subbiah, "My son, don't go to the Bhagavatar's house. He frequents *dasi*s (courtesans) in the temple." Subbiah's mother liked to prepare delicious dishes. It was a joint family and Shastri's brother Neelakanta Shastri lived in the house along with his family. Ganapati Shastri had only one child.

Subbiah woke up at 4 o'clock in the morning and left for the fields with his friend Viswanathan for his morning ablutions. Harikesanallur did not have the privilege of being situated near the Thamirabarani River. *Upanayanam* had been recently performed on Subbiah and he had to return immediately. He saw mother Sita milking the cow Lakshmi in the backyard of his house. People in the *agrahaaram* had woken up and the Oduvar (man who sings *bhakti* songs in the temple) of the Shiva temple started his morning hymns. While walking through the fields, Subbiah reflected on his conversation with his father. Looking at the rising sun, he remembered his father quoting the Upanishad: All this universe is born out of Bliss, by Bliss all live, and to Bliss all return. Delight, Bliss the source of life, the fount of this creation. Subbiah saw bliss in all creation, from the sounds of birds to the songs of farmers in the fields. "We worship God as Beauty, as Delight, Shyama Sundara," his father told him, "We should not be afraid of God, we should love him." Subbiah inhaled the fresh morning air and felt the cosmic vibrations, if you are awake, you can see the hands of God everywhere. He took bath in the Kannadian canal (or *vaikal* as they called it) and returned home and performed *sandhya-vandan* with his father. When the following *shloka* came, he stopped and admired the beauty of the verse:

> *sri keshavaya nama, apo hishta mayo bhuva, thana urje dadha thana, mahe ranaya chakshase, yova shiva thamo rasa, thasya bhajaya thehana, usathiriva mathara, thasma aranga mamava, yasya kshayaya jinvadha, apo janayadha jana, om bhurbhuvassuva* ।

> Salutations to Lord Keshava. It is well known that you Gods of water are the source of greatness in life. Please grant us the ethereal vision. Like the holy and dear mothers, grant us please the ultimate essence of happiness that you have. We are praying to you to possess that essence of happiness, of which you are the very personification. You gods of water should through knowledge help us to be born holy in the next birth.

His father understood why his son stopped midway and urged him to continue:

> *yamaya nama*
> *yamaya dharma rajaya, mrityuve cha anthakaya cha* ।
> *vaivasvathaya kalaya sarva bhutha kshayaya cha* ।।

audumbharaya dhagnaya nilaya parameshtine,
vrikodharaya chitraya chitra guptaya vai nama ।
chitra guptaya vai nama om nama ithi ॥

Salutations to Yama, the God of death
My salutations and salutations
To him who can keep in control his senses,
To him who is the king of justice.
To him who destroys,
To him who can put an end,
To him who is the son of Sun God,
To him who represents march of time,
To him who causes death to all beings,
To him who is supremely strong,
To him who is called the universal giver,
To him who has a bluish body,
To him who is being worshipped by all,
To him who has a huge belly,
To him who is really peculiar,
And to him who guards his secret.

akasat pathitam toyam,
yada gachchati sagaram,
sarva deva namaskara
sri keshavam prati gachchati

Like all the water that falls from the sky reaches the sea, all salutations done to all gods reach Lord Narayana.

Ganapati was a devotee of the Divine mother, the Devi, and was well-versed in the Shastras. He had all the qualities of an ideal brahmin. He performed *sandhya,* early in the morning, and collected flowers for the worship of Shiva. His *puja* was elaborate and not until he finished it would he eat anything. He never accepted gifts or anything other than milk outside. He would not even drink water touched by brahmins who took money for giving their daughters in marriage. For this strict adherence to the Shastras, the people of the village greatly loved and respected him. His wife, Sita, was totally devoted to religion. She recited the *Lalita Sahasranama* and *Saundarya-Lahari.* Ganapati, every morning, afternoon and evening, would recite the *Gayatri mantra* with intense devotion and faith. While chanting the *Gayatri mantra,* his chest became flushed and tears streamed from his eyes. In the morning, he would go with a basket to pluck flowers for the *puja*. The villagers had great respect for him and he was treated as a *rishi*. He was even known to possess miraculous powers.

He went on a pilgrimage all alone in 1837 to Kasi on foot, taking only milk and fruits during the arduous journey. He returned to Harikesanallur after a year and then went to Rameswaram. He slept in *mandapam*s and chanted the Lord's name throughout the pilgrimage. After these spiritual excursions, Sita became pregnant and gave birth to their only child, Subbiah. Ganapati sent Subbiah to a *gurukula* in the village at an early age and also took keen interest in his Vedic studies. Though Ganapati was busy in supervising several *yajna*s in the area, he allocated some time for his son and discussed with him religious and philosophical ideas. The child was also precocious and absorbed the best of Vedic traditions, displaying an insatiable appetite for scholarship in the Shastras.

15

"ACHARYA, why is my father leading such an ascetic life, depriving himself of all the pleasures in the world? The Bhagavatar is not like that. The poet is also a bohemian as I see him returning home in an inebriated condition," Subbiah asked his teacher.

"Subbiah, in all situations, we have to choose between the good (*shreyas*) and the *preyas* (pleasant). The wise man chooses *shreyas* and not *preyas*. The *Katha Upanishad* says:

> *anyach chhreyo 'nyadutaiva preyaste ubhe nanarthe purusham sinitah* । *tayoh shreya adadanasya sadhu bhavati hiyate 'rthadha u preyo vrinite* ॥

> One thing is *shreyas* (the good) and (quite) different, indeed, is *preyas* (the pleasant); having been of different requisitions, they both blind man. Good befalls him who follows the good, but loses he the goal who chooses the pleasant.

> *avidyayam antare vartamanah*
> *svayam dhirah panditam manyamanah*
> *dandramyamanah pariyanti mudhah*
> *andhenaiva niyamana yathandhah.*

> Fools, dwelling in the very midst of ignorance, yet vainly fancying themselves to be wise and learned, go round and round, staggering, like blind men led by the blind.

This is the reason why we require a *guru*. A *guru* helps us to discriminate between the real and the unreal.

> *ascharyo vakta kushlo'sya labdha*
> *''shcharyo jnata kushalanushishtah* ।

> When a wonderful disciple and a wonderful
> teacher come together, there is born great wisdom.

One student of Acharya Sankara said:

> There are many *gurus* who deprive the disciples of their wealth; but different from all such *gurus*, I bow down to the one *guru* Sankara who deprives the disciples of their sorrows."

"Who is a good *guru*, Acharya?"

"The *Vivekachudamani*," he replied, "states the qualifications of a true *guru*:

> *shrotriyovrijino akamahatoya brahmavitmah;*
> *brahmanyuparatah santo nirindhana ivanlah,*
> *ahetuka dayasindhuh bandhuranmatam shatam*

> Who is well versed in the Vedas, sinless, unsmitten by desire and a knower of *Brahman par excellence*, who has achieved tranquillity in *Brahman* who is calm, like the fire that has consumed its fuel, who is a boundless reservoir of mercy that knows no motive, and a friend of all good people who prostrate themselves before him.

I shall explain the difficult terms:

Shrotriyo : A true *guru* must know the spirit of the Shrutis; not mere letter, but the spirit of the scriptures.

Avrijino : Free from sinfulness. A man who has also achieved perfection in morality and ethics.

Akamahatah : He should not have desires. He must be free from selfish desires. His only aim should be to do good to others.

Brahmavittamah : He who is best among the knowers of *Brahman*, one who is merged in God so

		that at any point you touch him, you get only God out of him.
Santah	:	Totally tranquil; you cannot bring tranquillity to another without yourself being tranquil. His very presence is enough for the student to imbue eternal values.

"How does the *guru* attain this supreme knowledge? *Nirindhana ivanah*: in him the fire of desire has burnt itself out. He has the mind which has scorched all desires, which has become *aptakama*, *atmakama* and *akama*, the mind which has fulfilled all desires, which has *atman* for its content of desires, and which is desireless in every other sense, as the *Brihadaranyaka Upanishad* states. The *guru*'s mind is focused only on the *atman*. *Atmaka matve ca aptakamata*, by desiring the *atman*, man fulfils all desires. A calm mind is like a tranquil lake without a single ripple. When we throw a stone in it, this stillness is disturbed. Likewise, desires create disturbing waves in the lake of our mind. *Ahetukadaya sindhu*, the *guru*'s compassion flows like a steady stream to usher in tranquillity in the world. There is not an iota of selfishness in it. This love flows spontaneously. *Bandhuranamatam shatam* — he is a friend of all who come to meet him. Acharya Sankara asks us to seek such a *guru*."

"Acharya please give me *atma-vidya*."

"I know a great *yogi*, who has travelled throughout Bharatavarsha and just returned to our place. He is now in Mannaarkoil, I will take you to him. His name is Paramahamsa Shivahari. He is an Advaitic *guru*. He belongs to a saintly order consisting of realised souls who are indifferent to climate and live on food got by begging. He practised *sadhana*, which consisted of rigid discipline, for forty years in the Narmada Valley. He travels from one place to another on pilgrimage.

He goes frequently into *nirvikalpa samadhi*. Subbiah, listen to me. You are not an ordinary boy. Follow Shivahari and be his *shishya* until his death. He is a Paramahamsa."

"Subbiah" he said, his flaming eyes looking frightening, "Your parents will marry you off in a few months. You will be a *grihastha* (householder). Many *grihastha*s visit *dasi*s here. Some of them have gone to the cities embracing European education, and given up our traditional life. You are not an ordinary boy. The *Gita* says that all contacts are of pain. Desires are like raging fires. The fuel fed on them are the sense objects. You can never get joy by pursuing desires. No desire gets fulfilled; it only increases. Desire to enjoy objects of desire creates tension, anxiety. Your mind will be turbulent and will ask, "Will I succeed, or not?" Desires create mental agony. If the object of desire comes under one's possession, the mind will ask, "How long will it be with me?" We know that no object can be possessed by us for a long time. Even during the so-called enjoyment of desire, we feel uncomfortable. No happiness in life is unalloyed. The foundation of all worldly activities is sorrow. The joy in worldly affairs is compared in the Shastras to the cool shadow we may enjoy under the hood of a cobra. After getting the object of desire too, we are unhappy."

When Subbiah returned to his home there was a crowd gathered there. His father was calm and composed but his relatives were grief-stricken. "You mother has left us Subbiah," they said and it took some time for him to understand the import of this message. He saw his mother's tender face and wept; his friends consoled him. But he recovered soon and felt that the Divine had done this in order to prepare him for a higher purpose, a deeper goal. The funeral pyre reminded him of the burning desire in him to realise the Supreme. After the mourning period he told his father: "Father, I want to adopt *sannyasa ashrama*," His father was shocked and reacted slowly. "How did you take this decision?" "There is a call within,"

Subbiah replied. Ganapati Shastri did not know that his son had such spiritual goals. "I will engage a *pandit* for you to study the scriptures systematically. Why do you want to leave me? You know, you are my only support after the death of mother" he said. "God is there to support all of us," Subbiah said, "Kindly don't stop me. I want to accompany a Paramahamsa in his journeys and gain *brahma-vidya*. Please don't stop me." Subbiah took a small cloth bag and left the place. This was the last time he saw his father. Ganapati Shastri sat in his *puja* room and did *japa*. "Probably it is the decision of Shiva," he thought as a trickle of tears streamed from his eyes.

16

SUBBIAH took brisk steps to Mannaarkoil. He did not know the Paramahamsa. Why did he take such a decision? Was he hasty? He was unable to explain it logically but knew that the life he had led so far was over. He will not be seeing his playmates or relatives anymore. A chapter in his life was over. For the last time in his life the memories of playing marbles with friends, swimming in the river and having fun came, but they were overshadowed with his determination to know the Highest Truth, the Truth of Truths. The burning zeal to give up everything to know the Real kept him going.

He reached the outskirts of Mannaarkoil and stayed in a *mandapam*. He saw the beautiful carvings in the *mandapam* and thought about the days when it was first constructed, the days, as his father often told him, when people were obsessed with God. "The foreign rule is making us forget our scriptures and our people are enamoured of Western education," his father once told him. Subbiah looked at the stars and thought, "I will choose *shreyas*. Not for me the pleasant path. I shall burn this body in the oven of renunciation. I am not interested in this body made of waste substances." There was a *samadhi* of Kulashekara Alwar at Mannaarkoil. Kulashekara Alwar, the king of Travancore, renounced everything and lived as a saint in this area composing hymns in praise of Lord Vishnu. "Only in Bharatavarsha, kings have given up everything for the sake of spiritual pursuits," said his father. "You require a *guru* to teach you *atma-vidya*," his Acharya had told him. "Yes, I want a *guru*. I want someone to guide me," Subbiah thought, "I will not return. I have taken this birth for the Higher Goal." He slept soundly and had visions of celestical forces beckoning to him for the knowledge of the Absolute.

17

SANKARA Shastri says,

"Most people consider Acharya Sankara a philosopher and a spiritual master. But, as Swami Krishnananda says, he was also an unparalleled social reformer. He brought a permanent change in the outlook on human life. He was not only a metaphysician and a mystic but also a down-to-earth practical person. In spite of the social service organisations all over the world, we see only jealousy and distrust everywhere. We have social activities without the wisdom of life that a genius like Sankara had. The soulless outlook of modern life has led to soulless activities. Ethical, moral or social goodness is empty without godliness. What did Acharya Sankara do? He dived deep into the root of the cause of *duhkha* or suffering and said that sorrow is due to the absence of the divine element in human life. The divine element is required as the foundation of all human endeavours. Since we have banished God from existence, our endeavours do not succeed. We have become so egoistic that we lose the common sense to accept the presence of God in worldly life. What is the force that connects people? Why do people aspire for a better social order, one humanity, social peace, etc.? Where is the need for morality? Why should we be honest?

"Acharya Sankara wanted the people to understand that the transcendental or spiritual reality is a necessity for happiness and unity. He had a solution. His answer to the problem of mankind was the philosophy of the *atman*. He wanted to establish the existence of the *atman* as the universal principle behind the multi-varied world. The *atman* or the self is one. This unites mankind. This makes us connect with other human beings. This makes us sympathise with others; be affectionate; be duty conscious. The *atman* is the universal principle behind everything in the world. To live life is to live philosophy, said Sankara, and to live philosophy is to live in God.

"Acharya Sankara mastered the Vedas when he was eight years old, all the sciences and literature at the age of 12 and produced his masterly *Bhashya*s (commentaries) on the Upanishads and the *Brahma-Sutra* when he was 16 years old and left the world at the age of 32. He was both a philosopher and a scientist. He examined the causative factors behind every kind of conceivable or visible phenomenon. He never took anything for granted. In his writings he argued in a logical manner and stated his positions on facts and never on concocted things. Acharya Sankara based his philosophy on our own self. Our understanding of the things we observe is based on our senses, the body, mind and intellect, which are unreliable. The only truth is that we are. If we doubt our own existence there should be a doubter behind the doubt. No one ever says "I am not." Something is and that is the self. The self is that which knows but itself cannot be known by any sort of perceptional process. The self is some such thing which knows and which itself cannot be known.

"The self cannot be known through the sense organs. We have to go inward."

"But people call Sankara's philosophy *mayavada,*" I ask Sankara Shastri.

He replies, "Acharya Sankara is the most misunderstood thinker in India, though in his writings there has been total clarity. His logic was almost perfect. Vedanta clearly states that the *atman* is immutable and indestructible. Sankara states that the subject, *vishaya,* can never be the object, *vishayin.* Whatever is an object of knowledge becomes something other than the self. The knower is unknowable. The body, mind (*manas*), the intellect (*buddhi*) and the ego (*ahamkara*) are all objects of knowledge and hence variable. Therefore they are not the *atman*. How can the subject be the object? Our ordinary conception of the "I" is wrong and the true "I" is not the body, mind or intellect. It is unknown and unknowable. The *atman* is the eternal subject. It can never become the object. The individual is essentially the *atman*. The *atman* (self) is falsely identified with the *anatman* (non-self). Bondage arises from this wrong identification, but this can be easily removed. The Shruti states, "All knots of the heart are cut asunder, all doubts are removed and all *karma*s are ended, when the highest *Brahman* is realised as one's self." Sri Sankara declared that *Brahman* alone is real, the world is false, the individual is *Brahman* and nothing else, that is when we see the world without *Brahman* it is an illusion. We have to pierce through the veil of *maya* and understand that everything is *Brahman*. The Shruti states, "Thou art That (*tattvamasi*)." Sri Sankara considers *Brahman* to be *nirguna* (without any attribute), *nishkriya* (without activity), *niravayava* (without parts), *nirupadhika* (unconditioned and absolute) and *nirvishesha* (having no distinguishing element in it). It is pure consciousness. *Brahman* is both the *upadana* (material) cause and *nimitta* (efficient) cause of the world. Gaudapada, the *guru* of Sankara's *guru*, Govinda, says, in his *Mandukya Karika*: "There is neither dissolution nor creation, neither a person in bondage nor any spiritual aspirant, neither any seeker after liberation nor one that is liberated, this realisation is the highest truth." Sankara calls this negation of Time, Space, Causality in the being of *Brahman* as *paramartha satya* (ultimate truth). Sankara has introduced the terms *maya* (illusion) and *adhyasa* (superimposition). *Maya* the principle that unites contradictions is *anirvachaniya* (indefinable). *Maya* is also a nature of *Brahman*. We mistake a rope to be a snake (Sri Sankara calls it *adhyasa* or superimposition). The Acharya clearly states that it is *Brahman* that appears as the *jiva* through ignorance or superimposition (*adhyasa*). Due to *upadhis* (limitations) we do not understand that *Brahman* is the substratum of everything in the world. The followers of Sankara have given a wrong interpretation to the teachings of the Acharya and come out with the wrong conclusion that the *Brahman* has nothing to do with the world, that he was a *mayavada*, etc. The pots from clay are essentially made of the same substance from the point of view of the potter. The potter sees only the substance of clay in all varieties of pots. *Avidya* makes us see the different varieties of pots. Sri Sankara also introduces two other terms, *Vyavaharika Satya* and *Pratibhasika Satya*. That the world has no absolute reality and it has an apparent and relative reality is *paramarthika satya*. That the world has a reality of its own as far as practical purposes are concerned, is *vyavaharika satya*. When we dream, the objects of the dream are real while we are dreaming. Only on awakening do we consider them to have been false. The world is also relatively real until knowledge dawns. Then it is false (*mithya*) and *Brahman* is the only reality. Although when the world is seen without *Brahman*, it is false, yet it is not non-existent (*alika*) like the son of a barren women. He gives some reality to the *rajju-sarpa* (the snake in the rope) which he calls *pratibhasika satya*. Hence Sankara's theory is called *vivartta* as against the theories of *arambha* (of the Nyaya) and *parinama* (of the Samkhya)."

Sankara Shastri takes a book, *Day by Day with Bhagavan* and looks at a particular page in it. He says, "Ramana Maharshi has observed, "Sankara was criticised for his views on *maya* without understanding him. He said that (1) *Brahman* is real (2) The universe is unreal and (3) *Brahman* is the universe. He did not stop with the second, because the third explains the other two. It signifies that the universe is real if perceived as the self, and unreal if perceived apart from the self. Hence *maya* and Reality are one and the same." Someone asked Bhagavan Ramana Maharshi, that when the Upanishad says that all is *Brahman*, how can we say, like Sankara, that this world is *mithya* or illusory? Bhagavan replied, "Sankara also said that this world is *Brahman* or the self. What he objected to is one's imagining that the self is limited by the names and forms that constitute the world. He only said that the world does not exist apart from *Brahman*. *Brahman* or the self is like the screen and the world is like the pictures on it. You can see the picture only so long as there is a screen and the world is like the pictures on it. But when the seer himself becomes the screen only the self remains." *Kaivalya Navaneeta* has asked and answered six questions about *maya*. Bhagavan Ramana Maharishi has explained it incidly:

> The first question is: What is *maya*? And the answer is: It is *anirvachaniya* or indescribable.
>
> The second question is: To whom does it come? And the answer is: to the mind or ego who feels that he is a separate entity, who thinks: "I do this" or "this is mine."
>
> The third question is: Where does it come from and how did it originate? And the answer is: Nobody can say.
>
> The fourth question is: How does it arise? And the answer is. Through non-*vichara*, through failure to ask: who am I?
>
> The fifth question is: if the self and *maya* both exist, does not this invalidate the theory of Advaita? The answer is: it need not, since *maya* is dependent on the self as the picture is on the screen. The picture is not real in the sense that the screen is real.
>
> The sixth question is: if the self and *maya* are one, could it not be argued that the self is of the nature of *maya* and is illusory? And the answer is: No, the self can be capable of producing illusion without being illusory. A conjuror may create for our entertainment the illusion of people, animals and things, and we see all of them as clearly as we see him; but after the performance he alone remains and all the visions he created have dissappeared. He is not a part of the illusion but is real and solid.

In another instance Bhagavan says, "These names and forms which constitute the world always change and perish. Hence they are called *mithya*. To limit the self and regard it as these names and forms is *mithya*. To regard all as self is the reality. The Advaitin says *jagat* is *mithya*, but he also says, "All this is *Brahman*." So it is clear that what he condemns is regarding the world as such to be real, not regarding the world as *Brahman*. He who sees the self, sees only the self in the world also. To the *jnani* it is immaterial whether the world appears or not. Whether it appears or not his attention is always on the self. It is like the letters and the paper on which the letters are printed. You are wholly engrossed with the letters and have no attention left for the paper. But the *jnani* thinks only of the paper as the real substratum, whether the letters appear on it or not."

18

SHIVAHARI looked at Subbiah intently; he had eyes of fire. "Do you want to be a student of Vedanta?," he asked. "Yes, Swami," said Subbiah. "Then you have to be a *sannyasi,*" Shivahari said. "Come with me. I will test you for six months. If you pass the test I will declare that you are a Paramahamsa *Sannyasi.*"

Shivahari said, "*Brahman* is the only Real existence. There is no time, space, causality or multiplicity. Power, time, space and causality are created through *maya*. One appears to break into many. *Brahman* appears as a manifold of individuals endowed with form and subject to the conditions of time. *Maya* is the grand hypnosis, which makes the different manifestations of *Brahman* go through birth and death. The veil of *maya* has to be pierced for the individual to rediscover his identity with *Brahman*. When he connects himself with the eternal reality, he attains immortality."

Subbiah felt instantly drawn to Shivahari. "Here is my *guru*, I shall surrender myself completely to him," he thought. It was one of the moments in history when the self meets the self and the *guru* meets the *shishya*. The *guru* is nothing but one's own self guiding us through the cycle of birth and death. For Subbiah, he had seen his God. *Guru* is pure consciousness, the glorious *avatara* of the divine.

19

PROFESSOR Kapil Kapoor, of Jawaharlal Nehru University, addresses the students of a college in Madurai in November 2001. He states that, "Sanskrit has been completely kept out of the education system since 1947. There is a deliberate conspiracy to rubbish the grand Indian tradition. Ferdinand De Saussure, in one of his papers, argued that Sanskrit is the original human speech.

"There are two cultures in the world. One is Hebraic and the other is Vedic. The Hebraic systems are theocentric. Our systems — Sanatana Dharma, Sikhism, Buddhism, Jainism — are not theocentric. They are strictly monotheistic, monistic. We are Pluralistic and pluritheist. They say "don't give any form to god. Our one God is the one god. This leads to totalitarianism and intolerance. Our pluralism, pluritheism allows for tolerance and acceptance of others. It allows you to pick up a stone from the river and let you say that it is your Shiva. It tolerates everyone's God. But the Hebraic, Semitic religions — Judaism, Christianity and Islam — say it is one god and that too my God, not your God. It has to be my one God. You better accept it. The Jews did not have any proselytising zeal because they did not have a messiah between them and God. The proselytising systems are the predator systems. We are the fodder systems, we are fodder, the Parsis were fodder, the Jews were fodder.

"The computer is the god everywhere. It is merely a technique or method, but now it has become the object of knowledge to the great detriment of study and reflection on our tasks. We were always non-technological, theoretical people and produced great wealth of material. We are now swept away by the West which has given us toys to play with so that we abandon thought. In ancient India Vedic *mantra*s were taught. The emphasis was on good speech and not on writing. When writing came, the goal shifted to beautiful writing even if you speak wrongly. With the typewriter, speed became the goal and accuracy was ignored. Computer is trying to replace the mind. Imagine the amount of information stored by Panini in his mind for *Ashtadhyayi*! There was no UGC or computer or research grant in those days. He went to the mountains of Gandhara, went into deep meditation and in an uninterrupted *samadhi* produced rules one by one. We have given up this system. We have adopted the Western, observational, empirical and sensory system. The essentially oral *gurukula* system must be maintained. The *Gurukula* system cannot be replicated by the modern education system.

"What has modern India in the last 150 years created intellectually except implementing the borrowed systems? Any thinker or any new system? Nothing. We can contribute only if we work in our own tradition. But it is dying.

"Where is the support for our traditional scholarship? A Professor tried to sell to UGC the idea that it should give a one time block grant to a *pandit* in a village. "Put it in his account," he told them, "and then do not send an audit team. Do not send a UGC review committee after a year. He will have to put you up in a five-star hotel and give you good food. Don't do that. Give a grant and forget about it. Because, that is the kind of patronage that made that kind of knowledge possible." But then, I have not found anyone who can understand this that the only way you can preserve your knowledge system is to support the scholar so that he becomes completely independent of you.

"Moses says in the Old Testament, "Make no images, you have not seen him, images are the corruptions of the mind."

The idea must not be given a form, idea as idea and not as idol — this is the Hebraic thought. India has always been pluralistic in this respect. Advaita says that *bheda* is a construct of the observer, when you see more than one thing only then you see *bheda*. India, with this synthesising, transcendental thinking, offers an alternative to the Semitic religions.

"And, of course, the canards speak by the "Intellectuals" that India was never a cultural unit before the arrival of the British. The boy, Sankaracharya, born in Kalady in seventh century CE built a temple in Srinagar, Kashmir, which is still there and respected by the Muslims.

"That is how we are one in spite of being not completely like each other. We believe in synthesis. Our thought is transcendental.

"Mainstream education has uprooted us. Macaulay has been successful in culturally enslaving us, even after Independence. Our system of education has created a complete disjunction with our tradition of thinking. We have acquired a spirit of self-denigration due to it. Indian thought is also seen as old and irrelevant for these times. It produces a loss of self-respect. We have become uncritical receivers and applicators of ideas. Ananda Coomaraswamy used the term "educated Indians" and said that is how victims of Indian education are described! Bhartrihari (fifth century) says, "What does he know who knows only his own tradition?" That India was an intellectual superpower — internally, intellectually rich, with three very powerful *sampradaya* — *Brahman*, Bauddha and Jaina — and interacting with the then centres of learning in China and the Middle East. Today we have to change the statement to, "What does he know who does not even know his own tradition?" We have become subordinate to the West. They are the theory, we are the data.

"The European rule in India was different from the Islamic

rule. The Islamic rulers left us alone. The Western idea of man-centric world view has led to total conquest of nature. In the Old Testament it is stated "I have made this entire world for you to enjoy. All these fruits and birds and plants and trees and fish and fowl are for you to enjoy." Man is the lord and master. He is the chosen creation. Our tradition tells us that man is just a link in a chain of beings. A shopkeeper would, in India, refuse to kill a mouse and give him cheese. A housewife would get up in the morning, feed birds, cows, then the invalids, then the elderly, then the guests, then the children, then the husband and then herself. Human beings are part of the chain and you are linked to a superior entity. The laws are fair. If you are affected, it is your *prarabdha,* there is nothing wrong in the law. The idea in the West that man is the best being that God has created and everything is for man has led to self-indulgence and a producer–consumer society. It is a philosophy of comfort, individualism, imperialism. This created alienation, exile, depression, etc. In olden days in India, if a child plucked a flower, the grandfather would stop him and say, the flower is also sleeping. Trees are worshipped here. There was a time when people would not sell milk. The modern producer–consumer economics comes from the desire to eat more than what one needs. So you have pesticides, new seeds, all meant to exploit nature. Our concept of *samyama* does not tolerate indulgence. In the old *varna dharma* there was no money. Money is the greatest evil. Each individual did his allotted duty in the society and got his share of foodgrains from the common village panchayat. In Jainism, we have the concept of vegetarianism and *ahimsa*. *Niyama* in Mimamsa states that there are two ways of choosing something and we have to choose the path which does not do harm to anyone.

"In the Western system, it is survival of the fittest. There is no room for an idiot. Each one of our villages had an idiot. He was looked after by the whole village. If there was a handicapped man, he too would be looked after. If there was a *Harikatha* exponent or a *bhajan* singer he too would be looked after by the entire village. Food would be provided for them. Eternal progress is the myth of the West. Our concept is eternal return. The French revolution spread the lie that all men are born equal and introduced the right-oriented institutions. Since rights are directed towards your own self they create conflict. Our culture lays emphasis on *dharma*. The eldest son should not want anything for himself, he should always think of what he has to do for his father, mother, or brothers or sisters. *Dharma* is duty. It is directed towards the other. It creates harmony. In today's India nobody is bothered about his *dharma* or duty. People only talk about rights. Hence we see only tension everywhere.

"In the Western system, man is the master and the artist is a great crafter. In our system the artist is a *sadhaka*, a manifester. He manifests the unmanifested. The paradigm artist in the Western framework is Plato's carpenter. The reality in quantifiable, segmentable, measurable, changeable. It can be rearranged. Man is the master who rearranges it. The paradigm artist in India is the potter, *kumbhakara*. He has the clay rotating before him. He has his hands on the clay and there is a figure that he sees in his mind, a figure in clay. He shuts his eyes and lets the figure in his mind flow through the figure in the clay and when the two figures become one he opens his eyes. He has not measured or segmented it. He has merely changed what was non-manifest *dravya* (substance) to *rupa* (form). If he is dissatisfied with it, he would redo the process. He is not a maker. He is a devotee of the clay and the figure in the clay. His mind reveres the object. Beauty is not something of form or appearance but is in the object to which his mind attaches itself with reverence. In modern India we have been alienated from this reverence. These ideas are in the air and we have to tune ourselves to it in order to understand the strength of our ethos. Our concept of time is cyclic. The Vedic concept of *rita* emphasised harmony and balance. There is no self *versus* the other. Everything is the self. Adi Sankaracharya says — *brahman atam ekatva bodhena moksha siddhyate nanyatha* — Once you realise you are one with everyone and everyone is part of one in the large sense you are free from suffering. This transcendental outlook is the answer to pain and suffering.

"Indian civilisation has always been plural-civilisation — pluri-cultural — while seeking at the same time unity. In the *rasa* theory, after the eight *rasa*s comes the contribution of Abhinavagupta — *shanta rasa*. Bhartrihari observes that *ekatva* is superior — we have to rise from *bheda* to *abheda*. Synthesis is the grand aim of Indian civilisation. The pre-modern and post-modern have always existed in our society. It is high time we decolonised our mind and understood the strength of our culture."

Soon after the talk, I interact with Shri Kapoor and we become friends.

20

INDIA is *Bharata, Bha* means light and knowledge and *rata* means devoted. Bharata means devoted to light as against darkness. Bharata Desha means — devoted to the Supreme Truth. Bharata is Madurai, Benares, Rameshwaram, Ramanathapuram and Rishikesh. An Indian philosopher asked Socrates to tell him how life could be improved. Socrates replied that it could be improved through the process of inquiring about human nature. The Indian philosopher asked Socrates, "How can one understand things human, when one does not first understand things divine?"

I watch with fascination a discourse on the *Bhagavatam* and how children, teenagers and women listen with expressive faces to the various tales of the Lord. This is the Bharata that will always survive. In the internet, the sites on Vedanta and *bhakti* have proliferated. All over the world there is a lot of interest in Advaita. The people in the villages, towns and cities have the thirst for the supreme unknown. The desire for the ultimate truth which would in the end annihilate the very concept of desire has been sown by the ancient *rishi*s of yore. The foundations are too deep and the belief in the Ultimate so firm that even a thousand years of foreign rule has not made us forget the *Bhagavatam, Gita, Brahma-Sutra,* Upanishads, Puranas, *Mahabharata* and the *Ramayana.*

Shri Kapil Kapoor, who is in Madurai in connection with an academic programme, takes me to a five-star hotel where a left-liberal Professor is staying. Since he has a lot of influence in several universities, we discuss with him higher education. Shri Kapoor laments the neglect of study of Tamil, Sanskrit, Pali and Prakrit texts in mainstream education (at least in translation). We have abandoned the Sanskrit tradition and become prisoners of foreign idioms. The texts in these traditions cover all subjects and contain empirical wisdom gathered over centuries. Any effort to incorporate them is called revivalism and condemned.

"What is it, if not revivalism?," the leftist Professor asks over a glass of scotch. He offers us a glass, but we decline.

"What do you call," Shri Kapoor says, "the revival of classical Greek and Roman learning in Europe during the thirteenth, fourteenth and fifteenth centuries? Don't you call it renaissance or revival of classical learning? Then the same efforts in India are called "revivalism," "obscurantism." Why? No Western writer ever refers to Plato as "ancient" or Greek thought as "ancient." But when an Indian works on Sankritic tradition, it is called "traditional" or "ancient." People say here, "Panini the ancient grammarian." Nobody in the West calls Plato an ancient philosopher. This is because they are proud of their tradition.

"Our culture is totally different from the West. They say pre-colonial, post-colonial, etc. Their concept of time is linear, evolutionary. Our concept of time is cyclic. Our literary traditions are mostly oral. The author is anonymous. He is only a composer. Do we know the names of the *rishi*s who composed the Vedas and the Upanishads? The big "I" (or unripe "I" as Ramakrishna would call it) is totally absent. Here writing is a *sadhana*. A writer meditates and writes. Acharya Sankara has written a lot, yet there is no reference to himself in his composition or *Bhashya*s. In the West the humanitarian movements made the society man-centric and glorified individual personality. For us the ego is the greatest barrier, the imposter, who has to be removed."

"Have we not produced a lot of critics recently?," he asked.

"It is not," Shri Kapoor says, "Indian literary criticism. And what is this so-called Indian writing in English other than products churned by people in the metros. The UGC panels do not consider our Abhinavagupta, Anandavardhana, Mahima Bhatta, etc. as important. India's educated elite, the children of Macaulay, have been brought up to hate its own culture. The left, liberal, secular, modern people resist any attempt to introduce Indian traditions of thought in mainstream education system. They say that Sanskrit poetics is archaic, not suitable for India, merely theoretical, has no Shastra, metaphysically based aesthetics, and excludes non-Sanskrit oral literatures.

"Indian intellectual traditions have been continuous, without any break (unlike the West which witnessed vacuum after the sack of Rome). The words used by grammarians have become day-to-day usage in Indian languages. The theories are still used to analyse music and dance composition. Indian folk and oral art forms display the same continuity. It is very much a living tradition and no Renaissance or rebirth is required here. This continuity can be seen in the transition from Vedic Sanskrit to Classical Sanskrit, to Pali, to Prakrit, to modern Indian languages."

"Is not the tradition Brahmanical and elitist?" our *purvapaksha* (intellectual opponent) asks.

"Marxist intellectuals," says Shri Kapoor, "are always fond of attacking Hindu traditions. You people should read the primary texts. But you don't. Many of the so-called intellectuals abuse the *Manusmriti* without even reading it. They should read it, understand the social context in which it was written and only then criticise it or appreciate it. All the categories in Sanskrit poetics are analytical and descriptive and are not bound by caste. The three *sampradaya*s (schools of thought) are called *Brahman*, Bauddha and Jaina. "Brahmin" does not refer to caste but to the school of thought that upholds the category of *Brahman* (of Vedanta) as against Buddhists and Jainas. In our tradition we have place for Charvaka, Acharya Vallabha,

Acharya Madhva, etc. It is pluralistic. The Vedic *rishi*s said, *ekam sat vipra bahudha vadanti*. The truth is one; the seers call it by various names. Pandit Bhagavata Shastri said, Indian Knowledge tradition is timeless and continuous like the flow of the river. Knowledge has always enjoyed a privileged status in India. Acharya Sankara, who composed the *Bhashya*s (commentaries), travelled throughout India and addressed village gatherings in Prakrit to propagate Advaita Vedanta. Sanskrit was also a widely understood language in India He wrote beautiful hymns in praise of Devi. Acharya Ramanuja spoke about Vishishtadvaita in Tamil at the village of Melkote near Mysore to the people. He stayed there for 12 years. The illustrations and analogies in Sanskrit texts are given from day-to-day life, which is ample proof that knowledge was not the privilege of a particular community.

"Dharampaji in his book *The Beautiful Tree* has written about how strong the roots of our civilisation was before the British tried to destroy them. We have been fed with the idea that before British rule, we were totally uneducated. The book quotes from colonial records dealing with several villages in Tamil Nadu, to prove that people, regardless of caste, were well-educated.

"In the eleventh century, Islamic invaders vandalised the centres of Sanskrit learning and scholars got dispersed. Many of them fled to Kashmir and Kashi, which were known for Vedic learning. In the fourteenth-century Kashmir also turned Islamic. In the south, various kingdoms such as Vijayanagara, Chola and Pandya patronised Vedic learning. Many scholars from the north migrated to the south. But with the advent of British rule that too ceased. The introduction of English as the medium of instruction and establishment of Western educational institutions led to the closure of *pathashala*s and traditional learning came to a grinding halt. We Indians were led by the siren calls of Macaulay's ideology that India has no culture and its past was a foolish quest after false ideals and she has to change if it has to survive. Then came great people like Ramakrishna Paramahamsa, Swami Vivekananda, Sri Aurobindo and Mahatma Gandhi, who taught us the greatness of our past. We did have people from other cultures to help us. Zain-ul-Abedin (1420-70) was an enlightened ruler of Kashmir and encouraged Sanskrit scholarship. Dara Shikoh, the elder brother of Aurangzeb, translated the Upanishads from Sanskrit to Persian. Mulla Ahmad was a great scholar of *Mahabharata*. The European orientalists like James Prinsep (who discovered the edicts of Ashoka and deciphered them), Sir William Jones (Asiatic Society of India) and Prof. Max Müller did a lot of service to Sanskrit studies. Max Müller's greatest contribution was the translation of *Rigveda* with Sayana's commentary.

"The Vyasa *parampara* has witnessed the emergence of a long line of Vyasas in our history to save the Vedas and throughout Indian tradition texts have been lost, and they have been reconstituted and recovered. This is only a transitory period. The Vedas will emerge triumphant. I am sure about it."

Our *Purvapaksha* smiled mischievously and led us to the door without any comment.

21

SANKARA Shastri says, "For the study of the Vedas, *Sadhana chatushtayam*, or fourfold spiritual means is an essential pre-requisite. It is a must for self-realisation. The first one is *viveka* or discrimination. The spiritual aspirant should discriminate between the eternal and the transient. He should withdraw his mind from the transient world and not seek pleasures of the senses.

"The next quality required is *vairagya* or dispassion. Such rock-like dispassion comes only because of discrimination. The spiritual aspirant should shun all worldly enjoyment.

"The third part of *Sadhana Chatushtayam* is a group of qualities — *sama, dama, uparati, titiksha* and *shraddha*.

"*Sama* is mind-control. The mind must not be distracted by sense objects. It should consider them as transient. *Dama* is withdrawal of senses from their respective objects. *Katha Upanishad* states:

"Know the self as the lord of the chariot and the body as verily the chariot, know the intellect as the charioteer and the mind as verily, the reins. The senses, they say, are the horses; the objects of sense the paths; the self associated with the body the senses and the mind — wise men declare — is the enjoyer.

"He who has the understanding for the driver of the chariot and controls the reins of his mind, he reaches the end of the journey, that supreme abode of the all-pervading."

"In the *shloka*, sense objects have been compared to roads, senses to horses and mind to reins. The senses can disintegrate the mind. This is a recurrent theme in the *Gita*.

"*Uparati* is self-withdrawal. We have to withdraw from all enjoyments of the senses and cut all worldly bondages.

"The fourth element is *titiksha* or forbearance. When the mind is totally withdrawn, extreme climate like heat or cold does not affect it. Endurance is possible. There is no anxiety whatsoever.

"*Shraddha* or faith is the firm acceptance of the words of the *guru* and the Shastra. Intense faith in the *guru* and the Shastra leads us to the Ultimate truth. For this, restraint of the senses, focus of the mind, intense forbearance, is required. There should be no doubt and one should surrender totally to the *guru* and the Shastra. This leads to *samadhana*.

"The fourth and last element in *Sadhana Chatushtayam* is *mumukshutva* or intense yearning for liberation. Such people, with the grace of the *guru*, become liberated even while alive."

22

GANAPATI Shastri met his *Purvapaksha,* the Bhagavatar while returning from the vegetable market. "Greetings Shastriar," Bhagavatar said, "my son has got a government job in Madras. You know that he went to do his F.A. there."

"Glad to hear it," said Ganapati Shastri.

"Shastriar," the Bhagavatar said. "Why should we cling on to our ancient customs? Why should all the brahmins not embrace western education? Already I see it happening. The British will give us wonderful jobs it we do F.A. or B.A. It is high time we removed the tuft and adapted to the white man's ways."

Ganapati Shastri was visibly irritated and told his *Purvapaksha,* "bad days will begin for the brahmins, if we swerve from our *achara* and *dharma* and enter the field of competition in the pursuit of worldly things. Thanks to the able and saintly lives led by their forefathers, some brahmins are able in no time to outrun the other competitors and get the attractive things of the world. Such brahmins, who excel in the secular world, forget that they are misusing, ungratefully, the heritage of ages. In the beginning other communities will admire us if we attain success in the ICS (I am sure Indians would be allowed to compete in it in the future) and other secular jobs, but that will turn to envy and finally hatred. If the brahmins withdraw from the race to get secular jobs, they will be widely respected by the society. We commanded respect in the past not for wealth or strength but due to our strict adherence of *dharma*. I feel that slowly we will lose our respect in the society if we move away from our study of the Vedas. Bad days are ahead for us if we leave our *dharma*. Fifty years from now there will be stiff opposition to us and we will also degenerate in all ways. Already, land has done us a lot of harm. Some brahmins got a lot of land and they degenerated morally. Now this quicksand of Western education will see our end."

23

SHIVAHARI took Subbiah again to the ruined temple and said, "The truth is only one and this truth was pursued by Saint Uddalakha to Shvetaketu; by Yamadharma to Nachiketas, by Yajnavalkya to Gargi, to Maitreyi, to Janaka; by Vyasa to Sukha, by Vasishtha to Rama, by Rama to Anjaneya, by Krishna to Arjuna, by Sankara to Mandana Misra. It is: "Man's original state is Awareness alone. He is not either the body or the senses or the mind. The Awareness is as subtle as *akasha*, ether. Even though the Awareness seems to be within the body, yet like the lotus leaf on the water and the insect in the mire, it is not bound by it. Also, just as ether is the basic element which pervades earth, water, fire and air, this Awareness pervades the body and the mind and yet is not in any way affected by them. For this Awareness there is no birth or death, no bondage or release. That awareness is your real nature." *Yoga-Vasishtha* is a great spiritual work. It is there that the story of how king Janaka attained enlightenment on listening to Siddha's conversation is given. It is told by Vasishtha Muni to Sri Rama.

"King Janaka took evening walks in his royal garden, while his retinue stayed outside. One day Janaka, when alone in the garden, happened to hear the conversation of some invisible *siddha*s. The purport of the conversation is as follows:

(1) When the knower and the known become one, then the bliss of the self is experienced. This is known as self-knowledge and this is what one should aim at.

(2) To eradicate the *vasana*s one should contemplate on the self which bestows light on the seer, seen and the act of seeing. One should thus contemplate on the eternal

self which is the centre between the being and non-being.

(3) That in which this entire universe is established, to which it pertains, out of which it arises, for which it exists, by which it really is, that is the self-existent reality, the Truth. Let us contemplate on that in the heart.

(4) One should contemplate the one eternal self which reveals itself shining as "I." Instead of seeking the truth in the heart, the ignorant goes in search of God outside oneself. It is like a man throwing away the valuable *kaustubha* gem in hand and going after conch shells.

(5) The self can be realised only by those who have destroyed completely the host of desires, knowing the absence of happiness in the baneful objects (both in the past and future). Yet if one clings on to them one would remain in bondage and is no better than an ass.

(6) Just as the celestial Indra struck down the mountains with his thunderbolt, let us strike at the senses which raise their hoods as hissing snakes, with our powerful discriminative mind. By this the mind acquires peace, gets equanimity and becomes one with the Blissful self.

"On hearing the truth Janaka left all the affairs of the kingdom to his ministers and contemplated on the self. He said later:

"With the destruction of *sankalpa*, the mind will also be destroyed easily. The baneful root of mind being destroyed, the tree of birth and death will also be terminated. I have detected the thief who robbed me of my atmic Jewel, my self. His name is mind. I have been suffering for long due to this villain; I will now gibbet him and make him die.

"Till now I have not been able to bore a hole in the pearl of mind. Now I will do so and make a rosary of it by stringing it in the thread of experience and wear it on my person.

"The king withdrew and merged with the self, going into *samadhi*. After returning to the relative plane, he realised that the self was the substratum of everything. Rooted in the self he ruled the kingdom and became a *sthitaprajna*.

"Though there is a lot of chaos and confusion in manifestation, all that belongs to the realm of the mind — the ignorant mind getting split as subject and object. All experiences of life are relative, and related to the experiencer, who is nothing but a shadow having no intrinsic reality of his own. The reality in every person is the ultimate pure existence which is Awareness absolute that does not get split into subject and object. It is the only thing that matters. If the ego and all its experiences are dismissed as passing shadows, the ever-present ultimate reality alone shines forth. If one is even intellectually convinced of this truth, one will gain detachment and mental peace.

"We should experience this immutable and immaculate Awareness absolute which alone matters, which alone IS, despite the manifestation of endless variety of experiences.

"Acharya Sankara stated that the universe of names and forms cannot be denied in the day-to-day experiences for people who live in *avidya* (ignorance). From the standpoint of *Brahman*, it is totally non-existent. The mirage is a fact for victims of the illusion in a desert. It is like a man mistaking a rope for a snake in a dark room. Under delusion, the snake is real to him. The dream experiences are real to the dreamer. For people who have not attained true knowledge (*jnana*) of the self, names and forms are real. Waking experiences possess more reality than dream and snake. From the standpoint of *Brahman* it is unreal. The *jnani* knows that the self is the only reality. The cosmic illusion makes the ego and non-ego come into existence.

So long as a man is conscious of his individual ego, he is caught in *maya,* he sees multiplicity. He must perform his activities of work, prayers and experience pleasure and pain. Morality and immorality are realities for him. According to Acharya Sankara, the scriptures, spiritual disciplines, religion, and morality are based on *vyavaharika satya* or the reality of the phenomenal world. The transcendental reality (*paramarthika satya*) is that *Brahman* is the only reality. *Maya* makes one see the manifold universe. When the Absolute is known everything ceases to exist. The One appears as many due to *maya*. *Maya* is an enchantress! Understanding *Brahman* is the only goal of human birth, which itself is got through merit earned by good deeds. Without realising this, many waste this opportunity and slip down."

24

SHIVAHARI told Subbiah "Sayanaharya wrote *Vedartha Prakasha* (the meaning of the Vedas made manifest), his commentary on the Vedas. His brother Madhava Vidyaranya was instrumental in the foundation of the Vijayanagara Empire. His other works are *Yajnatantra Sudhanidhi, Prayaschitta Sudhanidhi,* and *Alamkara Sudhanidhi.* Madhva Vidyaranya, his brother, wrote *Panchadashi* and other Advaitic works. Ishvara Dikshita wrote commentaries on *Ramayana*. Appaya Dikshitar, who was also a poet, wrote commentaries on Advaita. His works include *Sivarkamani Dipika* and *Parimala.* Vallabhacharya was a great philosopher and wrote *Madhurashtakam*. All these great works emerged during the Vijayanagara Empire. I studied all these works at the monastery, apart from the Upanishads and the Shastras. Later my eyes fell on a *Bhashya* on *Lalita Sahasranama* written by Bhaskararaya who lived in Bhaskararajapuram, in Tanjore, for a long time. He was a Sri Vidya *upasaka*. I also took interest in Kashmiri Shaivism and studied the *Tantraloka* by Abhinavagupta and my main preoccupation these days is this great work. I want to go to the blessed village of Pallamadai to discourse on the saints of Kashmir. I want you to be my *shishya* and accompany me. I shall make you a self-realised soul. You will cross the *samsara* of birth and death with my help. I shall burn all the *vasana*s in you and you will become a *jivanmukta*.

"I belong to family steeped in Sanskrit scholarship and I was initiated into the Sri Vidya early in life. I have been doing Sri Vidya *upasana* for several years. I found my *guru* at the age of 12. He was a truly realised soul and was good at *mantra-sadhana* and he took me as his disciple. He had, through *tapasya,* acquired rare knowledge of Tantra and could converse with the *siddhis* of Kailasa. I accompanied him to caves to do *tapasya*. We never stayed at one place for long and went to holy *tirthas* where we performed austerities that would have killed any normal person. He wanted to bring about a renaissance in India and revive Vedic knowledge. He moved with untouchables and said openly that in Vedic times anyone could become a brahmin through spiritual *sadhana*. He was called a *muni* and soon a few disciples joined him. The Tantra deals with Shakti, the divine mother who sustains the world — She is Maheshvari, Mahakali, Mahalakshmi and Mahasarasvati and the *vibhutis* of the mother are endless.

"Shiva is the seer of the 16-lettered Sri Vidya, Maha-Mauna-Guru, Supreme Master of the silent ones. The *sadhana* of Sri Vidya leads to self-realisation, the realisation of one's self as the Goddess, the divine mother herself. It is the worship of *Sri Chakra*. The divine mother is primordial mother, the Aditi of the Vedas. She was One, became many with a thousand names. She is Rajarajeshvari, Empress of all gods and goddesses.

"The *Sri Chakra*, the *yoni*, source of all manifestation and the *muladhara* centre where *kundalini shakti*, the serpent power, is hidden and the *mula trikona* in the subtle body are awakened by Sri Vidya *upasana*. *Brahman* is threefold, *sat-chit-ananda*, Truth-Consciousness-Bliss. The worlds are three and life is threefold — *annam*, *prana* and *manas* — physical, vital and mental. The states are three — *jagrat*, *svapna*, *sushupti* — waking, dream and deep sleep. The forces are three — *iccha*, *jnana* and *kriya* — will, knowledge and action. The great goddess who goes through a threefold division is Tripurasundari, also known as Lalita. The divine mother is ever united with Shiva and is the cause of the universe. The *Sri Chakra* is the seat of all her powers.

"But, Subbiah, you need not get lost in all these. Knowing the self is like looking at your face in a mirror. The aim of Acharya Sankara was to revive the great Vedantic philosophy.

The Divine mother will guide you. Surrender yourself to the Divine Mother. Spend your days and nights in the study of the Upanishads. Do a lot of *dhyana*. The *Mundaka Upanishad* states:

> Just as the gliding streams, giving up their names and forms, merge into the ocean, so does the illumined one, being free from name and form, attain the effulgent, all-transcendent being. Verily he becomes *Brahman* who knows that supreme *Brahman*.

25

SHIVAHARI took Subbiah to Brahmadesham, where an imposing Shiva temple overlooked a Chaturveda Mangalam (village given as gift to brahmins by kings) and they stayed in a *mandapam* near the temple taking bath in the tank. Shivahari walked briskly, chanting Vedic hymns and sat at the *yajnashala*, invoking the Godhead of the Vedas. Immediately all the Vedic gods flashed in the mind of Subbiah and he visualised the *rishi*s communing with the deities. His consciousness got elevated and then an electric current passed through him, his eyes glistening like a *yogi* in a god-intoxicated state. "Shiva," "Shiva" — he said, recalling the supreme *yogi*. He had a vision of the divine mother approaching him and giving him the Shakti lance, with the background of the Rigvedic hymns in the sonorous voice of the *rishi*s. Gradually, Shivahari taught Subbiah *hridaya vidya* or realisation of the self in the Heart. As Subbiah walked out of the temple, he glanced at the Rigvedic *pandit*s getting ready for a *yajna* — I have gone beyond all this, beyond the Veda and "I" has ceased to exist. I am the eternal *atman*. He thought:

> In the innermost core, the heart
> Shines as *Brahman* alone,
> As "I-I," the self aware
> Enter deep into the Heart
> By search for self, or diving deep,
> With breath under check
> Thus abide ever in *atman*.

He recalled the verse from *Vivekachudamani*:

> Freed from awareness of any external object by reason of his ever being *Brahman*, consuming only what is needed for bodily

> sustenance proferred to him by others like one in sleep or like a child, looking at this world when he comes to external sight, like one seen in a dream, remains the blessed one enjoying infinite merit. He is to be honoured on earth.
>
> He is said to be a *jivanmukta* to whom there does not Ever arise the sense of the "I" in body and its organs and the sense of "this" in other things
>
> He is said to be a *jivanmukta* who is free from the sense of the "my" or "I" in the actions of the body organs and remains indifferent to them.

Subbiah looked at the stars from the *mandapam*. He had given some gruel to Shivahari, brought from a house by begging. It had now become a routine. They went from temple to temple and Subbiah begged from a house and gave a portion of it first to his *guru*. Shivahari was in a poetic mood, "The *purusha* is the self and the same self is in everyone. The *atman* is *Brahman*. The same *agni* burns in everyone which is nothing but the supreme *agni*, the real *Agnihotra*. The one is the many. King Ashvapathy Kaikeya teaches this secret to five seekers led by Uddalaka Aruni. Creation is infinite. It manifests a secret Delight. The Divine dream is an unending creative esctasy. We are Honey to the whole and the whole is Honey to everything. Cry *raso vai sah*! The *rasa*, the *ananda*, permeates into every activity in the world, creating a subtle harmony behind everything and everywhere. The *Brihadaranyaka Upanishad* says that this earth is Honey, this fire, air, sun, space, moon, this lightning, thunder, ether, *dharma*, *satyam*, this and these and all are honey. The *rishi*s with their *sadhana* realised this supreme, this *ananda*, this *Brahman*. Acharya Madhva in his *Rig Bhashya* wrote *bhashya* on 40 Vedic *mantra*s. He had also written *bhashya*s on Upanishads, *Brahma-Sutra* and the *Gita*. He points out the deep spirituality and mystic resonances in the Vedic hymns. Yaska wrote *Nirukta*. The *mantra* called "*Brahman*" was revealed to the *rishi*s by itself when they were doing *tapas*.

The *rishis* heard and saw the *mantra, sarvam khalvidam brahma* — they got a *darshan* of the Ultimate Real. The voice of God issues forth as a sound illumination (*cit-shabda*). The Veda and Tantra call this transcendental reality *para*. This (*para-vak*) is seen in a subtle manner inwardly (*pashyanti*) as an energising power (*pranasya pranah*) taking up a syllabic form (*madhyama*) and bursts forth into a sound (*vaikhari*). It is a pure expression of *Brahman* (*varnatmaka shabda*). It develops into a gross form as a gross diction (*dhvanyatmaka shabda*). Slowly the word enters the realms of language, meaning, and vicissitudes of history and whims of interpretation. The *vaikhari* moves a long distance from *para*. *Sadhana* requires us to comprehend the meaning of the Transcendental harmony of the Divine, getting rid of the scum that has collected in the long march of *para* to *vaikhari*. Again the *vaikhari* is still spiritual, degenerates into *anahata vaikhari*. Most people do not know the unperceived (*adrishta*) and unheard (*ashruta*) nature of the sacred word (*vak*). The real Veda, which is Shruti, is *para-vidya*, the perceptions and hearings of the *para-vak*: the luminous sound symbol of *OM*. The Veda describes the luminosity of the *para-vak* thus: it is a brilliance of multidimensional or infinite scale, flowing in a manifold splendour and invoking a thousandfold meaning. The *yajna* is the participation of the individual in the cosmic *lila*. The *yogi* is like Rishi Bhagiratha whose *tapasya* brought the Ganga to earth.

"The Veda declares:

> He who sees sees not, if he does not know the meaning of the symbol. He who hears does not hear, for his ears are blocked by the wax of misunderstanding. But Lo! For one who sees the light of Truth, it is like seeing his lady in her natural form of pristine beauty with no secrets hidden or to hide.

"Vedas contain divine revelations of rishis who did *tapasya* and got the highest Truth, the hidden secrets of the Divine of the Shaktis of the Cosmic Supreme embedded in the *mantras*."

They slept soundly in the night, and left for Rangasamudram the next day. Subbiah asked Shivahari to describe his spiritual experience after initiation into *sannyasa*.

Shivahari said, "After initiation into *sannyasa* my *guru* took over the responsibility of my spiritual training. As we moved from place to place, he got more disciples. We were once staying near the banks of Narmada. In the morning, when I opened my arms to pray, I felt a tremendous surge of happiness and my backbone became transparent. I saw my *sushumna nadi* which shone like a fire slightly dimmer. Then there was another fire, the *vajra nadi*. Then I saw the moon like *citrini nadi*, the *brahma nadi*. Then I felt the *ida nadi*. The tube of fire led to the *pingala nadi*. A voice pointed to me a beautiful lotus with four petals. It said — "see the *muladhara chakra*." A cobra inside it was lying in deep slumber. I knew that it was the *kundalini*. Then I saw the *svadhisthana chakra* at a lower level. Within the head I saw a lotus with many petals, with Sanskrit letters inscribed on it and I knew that it was the thousand-petalled *sahasrara*. My *kundalini shakti* was awakened and the serpent hissed, raising her hood. The petals of the *chakra* bloomed. I saw several Devi- Devatas on the *muladhara*. Soon the serpent became dormant. I went to my *guru* and was about to tell him my experiences when he stopped me and said, "I know everything."

"My *guru* had a special liking for me and I accompanied him to the banks of the Narmada while my companions were practising various *sadhanas* in caves. He said one day, "In the ocean of *Brahman*, I, the *atman* is a wave. There is no difference between the wave and the ocean. Acharya Sankara said that the *atman* is *Brahman*. Contemplate on *Brahman* — "I am a wave in the ocean of bliss, in the ocean of *Brahman*." Keep repeating this *mantra* —

I am the non-dual *Brahman* which is without anything like it,

> the beginningless truth, beyond all imagined distribution of "thou," "I," "this" and "that" of the nature of uniform permanent bliss and the Supreme Truth.
>
> I am not the doer, I am not the enjoyer, I am not subject to change; I am not the agent of action; I am of the nature of pure knowledge; I am alone (what alone remains on analysis), ever-auspicious.
>
> I am distinct from the seer, the hearer, the speaker, the doer and the enjoyer.
>
> So too, a man absorbed in *Brahman* remains forever in tune with his *atman* and sees nothing else.

"I wanted to meditate inside a cave in a hill. As I was about to start, my *guru* called me and asked, "Are you about to meditate?" I said, "yes." "I am happy," he said. I prostrated before him. He uttered the *mantra "om namah shivaya."* I went to the hill with my deer skin and meditated on the supreme monk, Shiva. I chanted the Dakshinamurti *stotra*:

I salute the Lord of Parvati who is tranquil, seated in *padmasana*, has the moon in his crest, has five faces . . ."

"I chanted *om namah shivaya* again and again. I felt a sensation between my eyebrows and beheld Shiva smiling at me and I was enthralled.

"He blessed me and left. I went outside, full of indescribable joy. When I returned, my *guru* also smiled at me and said, "You have received *darshan* of Parameshvara today." I was about to tell him about the event, when he again stopped me and said, "I know everything." That night I had a dream of Parvati and Parameshvara.

"I wanted to experience *Brahman* without form (*Nirguna Brahman*). After a week I went to the cave again and meditated. I focused on *Brahman*, determined to feel the Supreme without any form. I chanted the verses of *Vivekachudamani*, *Atmabodha* and *Tattvabodha*:

> That *Brahman* is without birth, growth, change, decay, disease and death, indestructible; It is the cause of the creation, preservation and dissolution of the universe. That thou art. Meditate on it in thy mind.
>
> That *Brahman* which appears due to delusion variously in the manner of name, form, quality and action and which like gold is itself unchanging, know that to be thyself. Meditate on that in thy mind.

"I entered into *savikalpa samadhi* and came out only after an hour. The sense of "I" vanished totally and I became pure consciousness. For a goldsmith all forms of ornaments are but gold and for a potter all modifications of clay are but mud. For me everything became *Brahman*. The world has existence only as *Brahman*. Apart from *Brahman*, it is simply non-existent.

"I again read *Vivekachudamani* and the following verses interested me:

> *Brahman* the Reality, is realised clearly, with steady certitude
> By means of *nirvikalpa samadhi* but not otherwise, for then
> Because of inconstancy of mental activity, the realisation
> would be mixed up with other notions.

"I went to the cave the next evening and started with *pranayama*. I concentrated on the middle of my brows and chanted the *pranava*. The *savikalpa samadhi* brought to me completely the realisation that I was the non-dual *Brahman*. I got a vision of myriad colours when I entered *savikalpa samadhi*. I felt intense bliss. Then I told myself "I am not going to experience bliss but be bliss itself." After an hour of meditation I entered *nirvikalpa samadhi*. I remained in that state for four hours. Then I came out and slept for a while. It was Ambal who first awakened my *kundalini* and it was She again who took me to the *samadhi* state. I lost all distinction of the experience, experiencer and object of experience. I was the self, the *atman*, the *Brahman*:

> *Nirvikalpa Samadhi* is that in which the mind becomes steady. Like a lamp kept in a windless place, and in which one becomes indifferent to (internal) objects and sounds on account of complete absorption in bliss.

"I was no longer the body, mind or intellect. With Ambal's grace I was able to remove the *upadhi*s (limitations) and realise that I was *Brahman*:

> But that man who rejoices only in the *atman*, is just the *atman* and who is contented in just the *atman* for him there is no duty to perform.

"I saw my *guru* waiting for me on the banks of Narmada, and he hugged me tightly when I went to him. Tears of joy came to me."

26

SHIVAHARI and Subbiah reached Rangasamudram, an *agrahaaram*, near the Thamirabarani. It was a settlement of *Yajurveda pandit*s and Vedic *mantra*s echoed in the place all the time. Subbiah begged, *"bhavati bhiksham dehi"* in the houses of the *agrahaaram* and gave the first share to Shivahari. "Guruji, you told me that you were in a monastery after the *samadhi* of your *guru*," he asked Shivahari.

"My *guru*," said Shivahari, "was extremely devoted to Sri Vidya *upasana*. He also told about Kashmiri Shaivism and the greatness of *Tantraloka*. He told us about Abhinavagupta and other Kashmiri scholars who specialised in Tantra. Acharya Sankara also went there and acquired his knowledge of Tantra. My *guru* told me to go to Kashmir, study *Tantraloka* and spread that knowledge in the South. Great Soul! He passed away in our arms, as we chanted Vedic *mantra*s requesting the supreme for the smooth passage of his soul.

"We started the monastery on the banks of the Narmada. We were five, Arya, Ajatashatru, Mahadevan, Mahendranath and myself. Among this, Mahadevan was the only other south Indian. Our goal was self-realisation.

"There was a deserted, dilapidated house, rumoured in the area to be haunted by ghosts. It was totally unfit for human habitation. There was a broken staircase in the west end and the entire house was damp and totally unsafe. The floors were damaged and the doors were fitted with broken wooden bars. We seldom noticed these inconveniences.

"We were immersed in meditation. We shouted *"jai shiva Sankara, jai shiva Sankara,"* hoping to be inspired by the supreme monk of Kailasa. We were intoxicated with thoughts of God. We cooked by turns, getting supplies by begging. I told my fellow disciples about the great Jesus Christ and the medieval Christian saints. I also spoke about the Upanishadic *rishis* and Acharya Sankara. We lit up a fire and I initiated everyone into the *mantra* of *sannyasa* and we vowed to devote our lives to the spread of the Veda. I gave them ochre robes and *rudraksha* beads. I spoke about the greatness of our *guru* and his austere lifestyle. We shouted — "*Jai Gurudev.*"

"We almost starved. Since we were *Sannyasis* we could not touch money. We went begging from street to street. We boiled the rice got by begging, added chillies and also the creeper which grew near the house. It had a bitter taste. The place was full of mosquitos and the water of the Narmada turned dirty during the rainy season. It was a trying time, but nobody minded. We were consumed in the fire of renunciation and the Vedic *rishis* goaded us to face anything. Most of the days there was no salt. Some days there would be nothing to eat and we starved. There were no leaf plates and we washed the floor and ate on it. We spent our days and nights in meditation and singing *bhajans*.

"We took turns and cleaned the rooms and carried water from the river. Arya was a good cook and he mixed the rice with the creeper and placed the pile on the floor or mattress. We had no quarrels, no misunderstanding. The ideal of our *guru* fired us and we kept shouting "*Jai Shiva Sankara.*"

"I took regular classes in Panini, Upanishads, and *Bhagavad-Gita* using the palm leaves of our *guru*. In the evening we danced with ecstasy.

"The most charismatic among us was the poet from Madurai, Mahadevan. We conferred on him the title Vyasa for his genius for composing poetry in Sanskrit and Tamil. He was born in Somnathapuram Agrahaaram in Madurai in a Telugu-speaking brahmin family. Their family had migrated from Chitoor to Madurai during the rule of the Naicker kings. He represented the cultural and intellectual depth of the small Telugu-speaking brahmins who came to the Tamil country, composed Sanskrit works, produced a monument called Thyagaraja Swami and *jivanmukta*s like Sadashiva Brahmendra, Upanishad Brahma Yogin, Ramabhadra Dikshita and Yajnanarayana Dikshita.

"Mahadevan was well versed in the Shastras and had memorised several *kavya*s. He could compose Sanskrit verses with felicity of phrase. He always invoked Goddess Meenakshi and said, "Mother Meenakshi is there for us." "The *atman* that is our goal," Mahadevan said frequently and recited verses from the Shastras. He read Valmiki and Vyasa and was writing a *mahakavya* on Goddess Meenakshi. He regaled us with stories of Madurai, its history and the kings that ruled it and quoted from the Tamil *bhakti* saints to show us the vast spiritual legacy of the Tamil country.

"Ajatashatru was from the United Provinces and enjoyed singing. He sang songs from Tukaram, Meera, and recited Tulsidas everyday. He was amiable and incapable of creating enemies, a true Ajatashatru. Mahendranath was from Bengal and was well versed in the scriptures. He talked about his village in East Bengal, and was nostalgic about the rivers Padma and Meghna. He belonged to Kishorganj in Mymensingh district of East Bengal and was picked by our *guru* during his tours there. He talked about Chaitanya and sang *bhajan*s.

"Arya was self-effacing, and though he knew a lot about the scriptures, did not talk much. He cooked for us and joined us in our spiritual activities.

"We wanted to burn our life in the fire of austerity. We thought of our *guru* who rose with the rising sun and meditated. There was always a divine presence in him. Sometimes he would cry: "O Mother Sharada," invoking the Goddess who resided in Kashmir. We lived in a trance-like state. We were in a state of divine madness and spent days in intense meditation. Arya spent nights counting beads. Mahendranath wanted to realise the Mother of the universe and did *tapas* in nearby caves. He also went to a graveyard in the area and meditated throughout the night there. Atmost everyday we followed our *guru*'s schedule of getting up at 3 a.m. and started our meditation. On some days the *japa* and meditation continued till evening. Arya prepared food for us or obtained it by begging.

"I woke up everyone in the morning saying, "Arise, awake, o ye children of immortality." Ajatashatru meditated in a small room and there was a glow in his body when he was lost in thoughts of the Supreme. Each of us was a flame. We felt that the Divine had chosen us for higher purposes. Ajatashatru's sonorous voice thrilled us and he entertained everyone with *bhajans* and *kirtans*. Mahendranath's mind also was a repertoire of *bhajans*. Mahadevan sang songs in Tamil and Telugu. He adored saint Tyagaraja and sang his *kritis*.

"We discussed the six systems of Indian philosophy in the evenings. We were deeply inspired by the life of Acharya Sankara who spread the Upanishadic message throughout Bharatavarsha. Though we did not eat much and lived in primitive conditions, we were immersed in thoughts about the Divine. There were cobras in the house but we never minded. We were busy in our spiritual endeavours and knew that animals never harmed those who practised non-violence.

"We branched out to different corners of Bharatavarsha with an insatiable appetite to see holy places and holy people. All that seems to be like a dream now. In those days postal service was in its infancy but we managed to get information about each other through fellow monks. Mahadevan went to Tibet and Kashmir. He died in Kashmir. Mahendranath went to Assam and became a reputed monk there. I met him in the Dakshineshvar Temple in the company of the Paramahamsa. Mahendranath died due to heart disease. Ajatashatru went to Tibet and practised meditation there. He became famous there. He died there. Arya died of leprosy, poor man. I saw him in a pitiable condition in Jaipur. From that group only I remain. Probably Master wants this body to survive in order to spread the philosophy of Acharya Abhinavagupta and Acharya Sankara. Glory be to our *guru*! Glory to the Divine Mother!"

27

SHIVAHARI took Subbiah to Srivaikuntham, a village nestled by the Thamirabarani River. They sat on the banks of the river and Shivahari said that a great saint called Kumaraguruparar was born in this village two centuries ago in the Vellala caste. He was born dumb. His mouth uttered the first words at Tiruchendur by the grace of Lord Muruga. The first words are called "Kandar Kalivenba" and the opening lines of the song are:

> You are verily, the knowledge
> That is beyond the comprehension of the celestial creator that dwells on the red lotus, Beyond the ken of the Vedas, ancient and divine,
> Beyond even the luminous principle of Nada,
> And, indeed, over-reaching even a knowledge that is pure.

"Saint Kumaraguruparar was the pearl of this sacred Thamirabarani River," said Shivahari, "which has produced a luminous line of saints including Shivagnana Swamigal who lived in Vikramasinghapuram. This river blessed by Sage Agastya is the glory of Tamil culture. Kumaraguruparar was destined to conquer the courts of Thirumalai Nayak and Delhi Moguls with his literary prowess and spiritual strength. He took the flower of Tamil Shaiva Siddhanta to Kashi in the north and established a *mutt* there. But that is later. In the beginning he went on a pilgrimage visiting the Shiva shrines in the Pandya kingdom — in Tirunelveli, Thirukkuttalam, Rameshwaram, Tiruppuvanam and Tiruparankundram. At Madurai a lot of Shaivite devotees hosted him in a *mutt*. He was enthralled to see Goddess Meenakshi and waxed eloquent about the goddess, depicting the divine mother as the divine child of the

Pandya king Malayadvajan. Goddess Meenakshi appeared in the dream of King Thirumalai Nayak and told him the saint Kumaraguruparar, who had encamped at Madurai, had composed a Pillai Tamil in her praise and arrangements should be made in the royal court for its exposition. The king rushed next day to the *mutt* where the divine poet stayed, conveyed the message of the Goddess and requested the saint to give discourse on his *Meenakshi Amman Pillai Tamil*. During the discourse Goddess Meenakshi, deeply moved, came in the form of the temple priest's daughter, sat on the saint's lap, took the pearl garland from the king's neck and decked the saint's neck with it. The girl disappeared suddently, much to the surprise of everyone, but the saint knew that it was the Goddess herself who had sat on his lap. The deeply pleased king mounted the saint on a golden throne and presented him with palanquin, horses, elephant, etc. Saint Kumaraguruparar stayed in Madurai for more time and composed *Madurai Kalambam,* a song in praise of Lord Shiva at Madurai.

"The work *Muthukumaraswamy Pillai Tamil* is a product of divine ecstasy and in it Lord Muruga's growth is described poetically. The poet says that there is no difference between Muruga and Shiva as seed and sprout are one and the same.

"The saint glorifies the Shaiva religion and also graphically describes the beauty of Madurai. Even the spiritual qualities of the tank in the Meenakshi temple are not left undescribed. The poem reveals the inimitable and majestic style of saint Kumaraguruparar.

"In *Meenakshi Amman Pillai Tamil* the saint begins by stating his love for Tamil. He describes the meeting between Goddess Meenakshi and Lord Shiva in Kailasa. This poem is full of references to the Tiruvilayadal story depicting the sports of the Lord, including the one in which Shiva worked as a labourer on the banks of Vaigai and got beaten by the Pandya king for negligence of work.

"From Madurai, saint Kumaraguruparar went to the Chola country and composed *Chidambara Mummai Kovai* at Chidambaram describing the glory of Lord Nataraja.

"Masilamani Deshikar of Dharmapuram *mutt* directed the saint to visit Kashi. This proved to be the turning-point of the saint's life. At Kashi, devotees thronged to him from far and wide. Hearing the fame of this saint, Dara Shikoh, the elder brother of Aurangzeb, invited him to the Mogul court. The saint went to the court mounted on a lion and with the grace of Goddess Sarasvati, spoke Hindustani. Dara Shikoh knew the Upanishads, he had translated them into Persian, and conversed with the saint on Vedanta.

"The Prince allotted a piece of land at Varanasi for the saint, impressed with the latter's spiritual strength. On the land, the saint started the Kashi *mutt*, where he delivered discourses in Tamil, Hindustani and Sanskrit on religion.

"In his songs, saint Kumaraguruparar says that he goes into a feeling of ecstasy, when he thinks of devotees like Sundaramurthy Naayanar, Sandeesa Naayanar and also the *Tevaram* hymns of Sundarar."

They meditated for several hours on the banks of the Thamirabarani and slept in the night in a *mandapam*. The next day they again moved to the river, after taking food in a choultry. The sight of the river in the morning elated the spirit of Shivahari who recited from the *Tirumantiram*:

> The earth is He, the sky is He! Well He be!
> The heaven is He, truest gold is He! Well He be!
> Sweetest song's inmost rapture is He!
> Him my love besought from heart's central core.

Shivahari said, "Agastya Muni is the chief of the *siddhas*. He is ageless and has been living in the Pothigai Hills for thousands of years. Several Rigvedic *mantras* are credited to him. When my *guru* travelled to the Himalaya he met an ageless saint who has been living there for 2000 years. His name is Mahaavatar Babaji and he reveals himself only to a select few. He told my *guru* that he was initiated into *kriya-yoga* 2000 years ago by Agastya muni. There was Bhoga Rishi. We had Arunagirinathar who composed the *Tiruppugazh*. He said:

O mind of mine,
Trust not the body
That infernal machine
Turning out pleasure and pain
Brahma who sits on the lotus
Created it to bind the mind.

O mind of mine!
It's good you decided to surrender
See Him on His peacock *vahana*
He has now taken charge of you
Doubt not there is no greater state.
Dwell on His holy name
Always, "Maindra, Kumara"

"Subbiah, see this set of palm leaves, this is *Tirumantiram* by Tirumular. He was a *siddha* saint. It is an ancient tradition. Lord Muruga gave the knowledge of Shaiva Siddhanta to Agastya and with saint Agastya starts an illustrious tradition. *Tirumantiram* is a treasure of spiritual wisdom. Just imagine! Saint Agastya walked through all these paths and is still doing *tapas* on the hills above. Lord Muruga gave him divine Tamil which he passed on to mankind.

"Agastya was a *muni*, a *rishi*. A *rishi* is a *kavi*, a "seer," whose mind rises to higher states of consciousness and invokes deities with his *mantras*. The Vedic *rishis* always kept the highest reality in mind and the Vedas came to them through intense *sadhana*. The same can be said about the great Tamil sages. The Veda is *apaurusheya*, there is no human author. Vedanta considers it *svatah pramana* — that is self-evident means of knowledge. The *darsanas* that spoke about *Brahman* existed thoughout Bharatavarsha. Let me kiss this sacred soil which produced the great saint Kumaraguruparar who worked for our Sanatana Dharma." Shivahari bent down and kissed the soil of Sivasailam.

28

SHIVAHARI said, "The Pandavas renounced the world, became ascetics and wandered through forests. Once they felt very thirsty. One brother said, "I will go and get water." He saw a brook nearby. There a *yaksha* confronted him. It would not allow him to get water unless he gave the right answer to a question. If the answer was wrong then he would die. As a result all the four younger brothers, after giving the wrong answer, died. Yudhishthira arrived and was shocked to see the corpses of his brothers. The *yaksha* asked him the same question. The question was "What is the most astonishing thing in the world?" Yudhishthira answered: "The most astonishing thing in the world is that though each and every human being knows that death is certain, people behave as if they are immortal." The *yaksha* was happy with the answer and as a reward, all the brothers were brought back to life. So Subbiah, life is very short and as Sri Krishna says in the *Gita*, very few yearn for liberation and among them, only a tiny number get it."

29

"THERE is an Upanishad called *Katha Upanishad*. In it Vajasravana is a pious brahmin who offers old cows to priests and performs sacrifices. His son, Nachiketas, asks his father to give him instead as an offering to one of the gods. His father gets angry and says, "Unto Yama, I give you away." Nachiketas, the *brahmachari*, goes to Yama's palace. Yama is not there. Nachiketas waits at the entrance for three days and nights without food. When Yama returns, he regrets having kept a *brahmachari* waiting for him without food. He offers three boons to Nachiketas. Nachiketas wants his father's anger to subside and greet him again with attachment. The second boon is the knowledge of the Sacrifice which would enable one to go to heaven. Yama grants both. The third request of Nachiketas is for the knowledge on death and the means to conquer it and attain immortality. Yama discourages Nachiketas from this request. He says "Don't ask for this. I will give you women, long youth and all the pleasures of youth, wealth, power but refrain from this request." Nachiketas is determined. He says that all these are ephemeral. Discovering the purity of the *brahmachari*'s purpose, his faith and pursuit of high spiritual values, Yama teaches him knowledge of *Brahman, brahma-vidya*. Yama begins by saying that *viveka* or capacity to discriminate the good from the pleasant is a primary qualification. There are two ways — *shreyas* and *preyas*. We have to choose *shreyas,* the path of good deeds and reject *preyas*, that of worldly pleasures. The spiritual path is not easy; it is like walking on a razor's edge. Nachiketas is a true aspirant, with a burning zeal to learn about *Brahman*. He wants the highest knowledge, *para-vidya*. He is not satisfied with even an offer of *Brahma-loka*. The

Bhagavad-Gita exhorts us to leave everything behind to obtain the highest knowledge — that of the Self. Even our stay at *Brahma-loka* will be temporary. Knowledge of Self alone will help us to cross the ocean of *samsara*. Nachiketas has chosen the way of the eagle and impresses us with his soaring idealism. Yama says that *Brahman*, the absolute self, is transcendental but when it is related to human existence it is known as *atman*. We are waves in the ocean of *Brahman*. Knowledge of the self alone would help us to cross the cycle of birth and death and merge with *Brahman*:

> The knowing self is never born; nor does he die at any time. He sprang from nothing and nothing sprang from him. He is unborn, eternal, abiding and primeval. He is not slain when the body is slain.

Ultimately we have not known that the self is there in us:

> Smaller than the small, greater than the great, the self is set in the heart of every creature. The unstriving man beholds
>
> Him, freed from sorrow. Through tranquillity of the mind and
>
> The senses (he sees) the greatness of the self.

The self cannot be attained through mere bookish knowledge. Intense *sadhana* and divine grace are required:

> The self cannot be attained by instruction, nor by intellectual power, nor even through much hearing. He is to be attained only by one whom the self chooses. To such a one the self reveals his own nature.

Lord Yama describes the human being, using the parable of the chariot:

> Know the self as the Lord of the chariot and the body as verily the chariot, know the intellect as the charioteer and the mind as verily the reins.
>
> The senses, they say, are the horses; the objects of sense the

> paths they range over; the self-associated with the body, the senses and the mind — wise men declare — is the enjoyer.
>
> He who has no understanding, whose mind is always unrestrained, his senses are out of control, as wicked horses are for a charioteer. He, however who has understanding, who has control over his mind and (is) ever pure, reaches that goal from which he is not born again.

"So, Subbiah, develop the spirit of Nachiketas, develop that fire inside you to know the self."

Subbiah's eyes were aglow with the Nachiketian passion. He looked at the mountains above and the Thamirabarani River and thought of Shiva, the *mahayogi*, sitting in meditation. From his study of Vedanta, he knew that out of *tapas*, the infinite creative heat of *sachchidananda*, manifests the world. The supreme self is the *agni* pervading everywhere activating the slumbering world to action. The supreme *purusha* resides in our body of nine doors and is the one behind the many. Knowledge of this self leads to eternal bliss absolute. Shivahari constantly pointed out Acharya Sankara's words, *ihaiva* — here itself. It is possible to attain immortality in this body, mind, intellect frame itself. "Nachiketas is my ideal," thought Subbiah.

30

THEY walked towards Tiruchendur. Shivahari sang Acharya Sankara's six stanzas on *nirvana*.

I am neither the mind, nor the intellect, nor the ego, nor the mind-stuff;
I am neither the body, nor the changes of the body;
I am neither the sense of hearing, taste, smell or sight. Nor am I the ether, the earth, the fire, the air;
I am Existence Absolute, Knowledge Absolute, Bliss Absolute — I am He, I am He (*Shivo 'ham, Shivo 'ham*)

I am neither the *prana*, nor the five vital airs;
I am neither the materials of the body, nor the five sheaths;
Neither am I the organs of action, nor the object of senses;
I am Existence Absolute, Knowledge Absolute, Bliss absolute — I am He, I am He (*Shivo 'ham, Shivo 'ham*)

I have neither aversion nor attachment, neither greed nor delusion;
Neither egotism nor envy, neither dharma nor *moksa*;
I am neither desire nor objects of desire;
I am Existence Absolute, Knowledge Absolute, Bliss Absolute — I am He, I am He (*Shivo 'ham, Shivo 'ham*)

I am neither sin nor virtue, neither pleasure nor pain;
Nor temple nor worship, nor pilgrimage nor scripture,
Neither the act of enjoying, the enjoyable nor enjoyer;
I am Existence Absolute, Knowledge Absolute, Bliss Absolute, — I am He, I am He (*Shivo 'ham, Shivo 'ham*)

I have neither death nor fear of death, nor caste;
Nor was I ever born, nor had I parents, friends and relations;

I have neither *guru*, nor disciple;

I am Existence Absolute, Knowledge Absolute, Bliss Absolute — I am He, I am He (*Shivo 'ham, Shivo 'ham*)

I am untouched by the senses. I am neither *mukti* nor knowable;

I am without form, without limit, beyond space, beyond time;

I am in everything; I am the basis of the universe; everywhere am I.

I am Existence Absolute, Knowledge Absolute, Bliss Absolute — I am He, I am He (*Shivo 'ham, Shivo 'ham*)

Soon after finishing the song, Shivahari went into *nirvikalpa samadhi*. He remained in that state for five hours. Subbiah had already been instructed by his *guru* regarding this state and he waited for the master to return to the *sahaja* state.

On the way a Mudaliar woman was cooking food in a hut. Shivahari told the woman that he was hungry and requested her to provide food. Seeing the tall saint, with matted locks and strings of beads, the woman was surprised.

"Swami, will you take food from us? I am not a brahmin," she said. "Mother," Shivahari addressed her, "I am a Paramahamsa *sannyasi*. I have no caste." She provided food which both Shivahari and Subbiah ate with great relish. They slept under a tree. The midday sun was hot.

While walking through the road, Shivahari said to Subbiah, "My boy, your goal should be self-realisation. That is the aim of our existence. Remain vigilant while you are on the spiritual path. May the Divine Mother guide you. The first step is surrender. That would lead to *atma-vichara*. The body is a result of *karma*. It is not under one's control. Prompted by the sense of being the doer, people act like the statue that appears to carry the weight of a temple tower.

"Thayumanavar said, "Sometimes I think that all actions

are only yours and not mine. When deluded by *maya*, I identify actions as mine. Then I remain without thought of any action. O Sachchidananda Guru! Ordain that all actions become yours so that this mad one attains the blessed state."

He further said: "To those who knew the secret that all is your doing, you gave unlimited bliss. To me, a base covetous dog, you ordained this other way. O qualified one! To whom can I go to complain about the weakness of mind?

Thayumanavar also said: "There are no actions that can be classified as "mine." It is only proper to say all actions are Yours alone. I have made over to you my body, possessions and soul. It is for you to remove the impurities that abound in my mind and bestow your grace in whatever way you think fit!"

Shivahari said, "The *Tevaram* states: "Only those who give up caring for the body and who delight in You will know (You)."

"Now, Subbiah, I will tell you about *Ribhu Gita*. Ribhu taught his disciple Nidagha about the supreme truth of the one Absolute Reality without a second. Nidagha was reluctant to follow this path. He settled in his native town to devote his life to rituals and ceremonies.

"Since Ribhu loved his disciple, he went in the disguise of a village rustic. Nidagha was watching a royal procession. "What's happening here?" Ribhu under the guise of the rustic asked Nidagha. "The King is going in procession," replied the unsuspecting Nidagha. "O! It is the king. He goes in procession? But where is he?" asked the rustic. "There, on the elephant," said Nidagha. "You say the king is on the elephant. Yes I see the two," said the rustic, "But which is the king and which is the elephant?" "What!" exclaimed Nidagha. "You see the two, but do not know that the man above is the king, and the animal below is the elephant? What is the use of talking to a man like you?" "Pray be not impatient with an ignorant man like me," said the rustic, "But you said "above" and "below" — what do you mean?" Nidagha got irritated. He said, "You see the king and the elephant, the one above and the other below. Yet you want to know what is meant by "above" and "below?" If action alone can teach you, then bend forward." Nidagha got on the shoulder of the rustic and said, "You see now. I am above as the king, you are below as the elephant. Is that clear?" The rustic said, "Not yet. You say you are above like the king, and I am below, like the elephant. The "king" the "elephant" "above" and "below" so far it is clear. But please tell me what you mean by "I" and "you"?" At once Nidagha realised that the rustic would only be his *guru*. He fell at his feet and said, "Who else but my venerable master, Ribhu, could have thus drawn my mind from duality and the superficialities of physical existence to the true being of the self? O! benign Master, I crave thy blessings." Here are a few verses from the *Ribhu Gita*." Taking an old palm leaf from his jute bag, Shivahari read:

"The concept "I am the body" is created by the sentient inner organ, the mind. It is also the illusive bondage to identification with birth and death. It is the source of all groundless fears. If there is no trace of it at all everything will be found to be the reality of the Supreme Absolute Being."

At Tiruchendur, Shivahari shouted "Subramanya, Subramanya," seeing the image of Lord Muruga and went into *samadhi*. They left the holy town that evening and walked towards Kallidaikurichi. While walking Shivahari quoted Appaya Dikshitar, "Just as a court-dancer dancing in front of the king cannot stop till the king makes a gesture to do so, even though the dancer's legs ache, O Lord, I am dead tired of having taken so many births and deaths. One glance of grace from you is enough to put an end to the dance of my births and deaths; please grant that to me." "Subbiah, the aim of human birth is to meditate on *Brahman* through the several steps that the Shastra prescribes. Pray to the Divine Mother. As a *guru*, I will show you the way," said Shivahari.

31

No sooner had they reached the Kannadian Canal than it rained heavily. Shivahari quickly went near a hut near the canal along with Subbiah. There was a family inside, including children. The only man, turbaned, came out. "Can we stay with you tonight, sir," Shivahari asked the man. The man said, "I am a sweeper, an untouchable, Swami." Shivahari replied, "I am a Paramahamsa *sannyasi*. I am beyond caste. This is my disciple, Subbiah." "But Swami, what will the society say?" the man said. "Sir, I have travelled throughtout Bharatavarsha. In Calcutta, I often visited a great saint called Ramakrishna Paramahamsa. He got up one midnight, went to the house of a *chandala* and washed his latrine, without the knowledge of the untouchable. Had the latter known this, he would have objected. Such are our people. The high born assumes arrogance. The so-called low-born knows that he is inferior. That is the tragedy of our country. While cleaning, Ramakrishna was praying to the Divine Mother: "O Mother! Make me the servant of the pariah; make me feel that I am lower than the pariah." "Then Swami it is alright. Welcome to this poor man's hut," said the man. "We assure you that we take only gruel and no meat." Shivahari and Subbiah took gruel and bananas for dinner. They slept soundly in a corner of the hut.

32

Thanking the man, they continued their journey. "Look, Subbiah there is a village nearby," said Shivahari. "Let us stay there for a day." They entered the village. It was a settlement of brahmins. A group of brahmins told the pair, "Stop!"

"Don't come near us. We learnt that you don't follow caste rules. You stay with untouchables, eat with them and sleep in their huts. Don't enter this village," they said.

Shivahari said, "Learned brahmins, Salutations! I have a lot of respect for you. I am a Paramahamsa *sannyasi*. This is my disciple. I am beyond caste rules."

"No, we don't want such people here," said a person in the group.

"Shame on you brahmins," said a visibly angry Shivahari, "Do you know about an incident in the life of Sankaracharya? It is there in *Sankara Digvijaya* by Madhava Vidyaranya. Taking a palm leaf from his bag, Shivahari read:

> Once upon a time, when the great Acharya (Sankaracharya) was on his way to the holy salvation-offering Kashi, he saw on the road Shiva with his consort Gauri in the guise of Chandala, and said, "Get away, get away!" The Chandala Sankara (Shiva) in turn spoke to (Acharya) Sankara.

"The Chandala speaks:

> O worthy brahmin, please let me know what exactly you wish to keep away. Is it the physical body from another body, or consciousness from another consciousness?
>
> Is there any difference between the reflection of the sun in the waters of the Ganga and that in the water flowing by the

chandala's hut or between the space within a golden jar and that within a clay pot? Wherefrom has arisen this great delusion, which sees one as a brahmin and another as a *chandala*, in this inner self — this one waveless ocean of self-existing bliss and consciousness?

"Acharya Sankara gives his reply in five verses of *Manisha Panchakam*:

> That consciousness which shines forth most distinctly in waking, dream and deep sleep; that which is the one witness of the universe that threads all bodies ranging from Brahma's down to the ant's; that I am and not anything phenomenal — whoever possesses this firm wisdom is my *guru*, be he a *chandala* or a person twice-born. This is my conviction.
>
> I and this whole universe are but *Brahman*, a manifestation of pure consciousness; all these phenomena have been imagined by me through ignorance comprising the three *gunas*. He whose mind is thus firmly rooted in the supremely blissful, eternal, pure, transcendental reality is my *guru*, be he a *chandala* or a person twice-born. This is my conviction.
>
> One who having realised, through the instructions of the guru, the utter unreality of the whole universe, engages oneself in the contemplation of the eternal *Brahman* with an honest calm mind, and burns up all sins, past and future, in the fire of consciousness — (such a person) has submitted the body to *prarabdha karma*. This is my conviction.
>
> The *yogi* whose mind is tranquil due to constant contemplation on the effulgence of pure consciousness existing in lower animals, humans, and gods as the "I" within; by whose lustre shine forth the mind, the senses, the body, and the objects of the senses all void of consciousness in themselves; and which, like the sun, is covered by the very objects that it illumines — such a person is my *guru*. This is my conviction.
>
> He whose mind is merged in that eternal ocean of Bliss — even the small part of a drop of which satisfies Indra and

> others realising which, through a totally unagitated mind, a sage becomes happy — such a person is himself *Brahman* and not (a mere) knower of *Brahman*. He is a worthy soul at whose feet the best of the gods bow down. This is my conviction.

"O worthy brahmins, the *Vajrasucika Upanisad*," said Shivahari, which is a part of *Samaveda* states:

> The brahmin, the kshatriya, the vaishya and the shudra are the four *varna*s (classes). That the brahmin is the chief among these classes is in accord with the Vedic texts and is affirmed by the Smritis. In this connection there is a point worthy of investigation: who is, verily, the brahmin? Is he the individual soul? Is he the knowledge? Is he the deeds? Is he the performer of the rites?
>
> Of these if the first position that the *jiva* or the individual soul is brahmin, it is not so; for the individual's form is one and same in the large number of previous and prospective bodies. Even though the *jiva* (individual soul) is one, there is scope for many bodies due to the stress of *karma*, and in all these bodies the form of the *jiva* is one and the same. Therefore the *jiva* is not the brahmin.
>
> Then if it is said that the body is the brahmin, it is not so, because of the oneness of the nature of the body which is composed of the five elements in all cases of human beings down to the outcastes. Therefore, the body is not the brahmin.
>
> Then if it is said that birth makes the brahmin, it is not so, many sages are of diverse origin. We hear from the sacred books that Rishyashringa was born of a deer, Kaushika of *kuśha* grass, Jambuka from a jackal, Valmiki from an anthill, Vyasa from a fisher girl, Gautama from the back of a hare, Vasishtha from Urvashi (the celestial nymph), Agastya from an earthern jar. Among these, despite their birth, there are many sages, who have taken the highest rank, having given proof of their wisdom. Therefore birth does not make a brahmin.

> Then if it is said that knowledge makes a brahmin, it is not so because among kshatriyas and others there are many who have seen the Highest Reality and attained wisdom. Therefore knowledge does not make a brahmin.

"In the end you have the definition of a brahmin," said Shivahari. It states:

> Then who verily is the brahmin? He who, after directly perceiving like the *amalaka* fruit in the palm of one's hand, attribute and action, devoid of all faults such as the six infirmities and the six states, of the form of truth, wisdom, bliss and eternity, that is by itself, devoid of determinations the basis of endless determinations, who functions as the indwelling spirit of all beings, who pervades the interior and the exterior of all, like ether, of the nature of bliss, indivisible, immeasurable, realisation only through one's experience and who manifests himself directly (as one's self) and through the fulfilment of his nature, becomes rid of the faults of desire, attachment, etc., and states of being, spite, greed, expectation, bewilderment, etc., with his mind unaffected by ostentation and the like, he lives. He alone who is possessed of these qualities is the brahmin. This is the view of the Vedic texts and tradition, ancient lore and history. The accomplishment of the state of the brahmin is otherwise impossible. Meditate on *Brahman*, the self who is being, consciousness and bliss, without a second, meditate on *Brahman*. . . .

"O worthy, brahmins, Mother Shruti itself repudiates the idea that one is a brahmin by birth. Have you heard of the *Vyadha Gita*? Vyadha means butcher. It is there in the *Mahabharata*. A brahmin *sannyasi* is meditating in a forest. He is disturbed by the droppings of a bird. He stares at the bird and it drops down dead. He goes to the village to beg for alms. He asks for food in front of a house. Since the housewife inside is attending to her sick husband, she asks him to wait.

"The *sannyasi* gets angry and thinks, "You wretched woman, how dare you make me wait! You do not know my power yet." The housewife immediately says, "I am neither a crow nor a crane to be burnt." The *sannyasi* is amazed. He asks her, "How do you know about the bird?" The housewife replies: "I don't practise any austerity or penance. I do my duty with cheerfulness and wholeheartedness and through *karma-yoga* I got the powers to read your mind. If you have questions on dharma, you can meet a *dharma vyadha* (righteous butcher) in the town of Mithila."

"The *sannyasin* reaches Mithila and inside the market sees a corpulent *vyadha* cutting meat and bargaining. The *sannyasin* is totally surprised. "How could you become enlightened after doing such filthy, ugly work?" he asks. The *vyadha* replies, "No duty is ugly or impure. All work must be done by dedicating it to God and with total detachment. The highest good can be achieved by the two main pillars of *dharma, ahimsa* (non-violence) and *satya* (truth). Stick to the course of action that leads to the highest good of all beings and you will get the answer to all your doubts. Not birth but *dharma* and virtuous conduct makes one a brahmin."

"O learned brahmins, have you heard about the story of Satyakama in *Chhandogya Upanishad*?" asked Shivahari.

"Once upon a time Satyakama Jabala addressed his mother Jabala, "Mother, I desire to live the life of a student of sacred knowledge. Of what family am I?"

"Then she said to him, "I do not know, my child, of what family you are. In my youth, when I went about a great deal, as a maid servant, I got you. So I do not know of what family you are. However, I am Jabala by name and you are Satyakama by name. So you may speak of yourself as Satyakama Jabala.

"Satyakama informs this to Gautama Rishi and says "I wish to become a student of sacred knowledge. May I become your pupil, venerable, sir?" Gautama Rishi was impressed with the lad's truthful nature and said, "None but a brahmin could thus explain. I will receive you as a pupil. Thou hast not departed from the truth."

"The *yaksha* in *Mahabharata* asked Yudhishthira, "Who is a brahmin? One who studied the Veda, or one who is born a brahmin?" "Neither," replied Yudhishthira, "The true brahmin is he whose life is pure." Again in another part of Vyasa's epic Yudhishthira tells a Python, "He who speaks the truth, who is patient, and is compassionate, whose character is without any blemish, who gives alms, he is a brahmin." The Python asks him, "What if a shudra has these qualities?" Without any hint of hesitation, Dharmaraja replies, "A shudra who has these qualities is not a shudra and if a brahmin does not have these qualities, he is certainly not a brahmin. I am convinced that it is not birth that determines the caste to which one belongs, but it is the character that decides. In my opinion, it is the holy Gayatri who is the true mother of a brahmin, and the teacher who is the true father. Thus that person is a real brahmin who has studied the Vedas, whose character is without blemishes, who strives to realise the *Brahman*, the supreme entity."

"Hence O brahmins," said Shivahari, "see the indwelling self as common to all. *Brahman* is the only reality. Just as the goldsmith sees all varieties of ornaments as ones made of gold, *Brahman* is the substratum of this world. Names and forms are due to *maya*. Examine the origin of the *rishis*."

The brahmins of the village bowed to the Paramahamsa. "We didn't know that you were a realised soul. Forgive us. Please partake of food with us." They felt guilty that they had insulted such a great saint.

33

SUBBIAH and Shivahari moved from one village to another. Shivahari liked Rangasamudram in particular and went there again and again. It was a village of Vedic scholars and each house had an *agnihotra*. The Vedic chants resonated everywhere in the village. Shivahari and Subbiah stayed in the cattle shed and meditated on the self. They took rest in a *mandapam* near Rangasamudram. A *ganapadigal* was reading the *Mahabharata* to a group of eager listeners. Shivahari admired the sight and said to Subbiah, "Look at that, Subbiah. Our Sanatana Dharma will survive so long as such enthusiastic people are there to spread the religion to the masses. Look at the way in which he translates each word of Vyasa into Tamil and dishing it out to the eager audience. Vyasa was a supreme artist and could create verbal pictures with his rich vocabulary. We have to take our *dharma* to the masses. The Alwars wrote in Tamil profound religious poetry and took our *dharma* to the common people. The Buddha also was a great religious and social reformer. He created a revolution by preaching *jnana* to the masses."

In the evening they proceeded to Krishnan Koil Street in Amabasamudram where Shivahari wanted to meet a Vaishnavite scholar. The street was full of Vaishnavites who got up well before sunrise to go to the Thamirabarani, take bath and after sporting *namam* (caste-mark) performed the *pratah-sandhya* (morning *sandhya*) prayers and other rituals. They returned home and taught Vedas to the boys, an activity which went on till 12:00 noon. Then, they went to the river again, took bath and performed *madhyahnika* (afternoon *sandhya*) prayers. They returned home and the head of the family did *Tiruvaradhanam*. The rest of the household recited Thiruvaimozhi and offered *naivedyam* (offering) to Lord Vishnu; it is only after the *puja* which finished at one thirty in the afternoon that the Vaishnavite brahmins had the first meal of the day. Lunch was served on banana leaves or stitched leaves and after lunch the elders took rest. The youngsters were taught in the afternoon arithmetic, Thiruvaimozhi, Sanskrit Logic, etc. In the evening they again went to the river for bath and *sayam-sandhya* (evening *sandhya*) prayers, returned home, recited *shloka*s and then took their dinner. The *Agnihotra* was maintained throughout the day. Even though only boys were taught the Vedas the women overheard them, knew to recite them and whenever the teacher was absent the ladies corrected the pronunciation of the Vedic recitation of the boys. Some of the women knew the entire Thiruvaimozhi running into 4,000 verses by heart. Subbiah felt that every occupant of that *agrahaaram* of Vaishnavite brahmins was Lord Vishnu himself.

Shivahari conversed with Rangaswami Iyengar, a tall gentleman with a big tuft, on the *Brahma-Sutra-Bhashya* of Acharya Ramanuja. Iyengar was impressed by Shivahari's knowledge of the *Sri Bhashya* of Acharya Ramanuja.

Shivahari said to Subbiah, "Bharatavarsha has always witnessed the arrival of messengers of the spirit to save Sanatana Dharma and this *parampara* includes Acharya Sankara, Acharya Ramanuja, Acharya Madhva and the Paramahamsa of the Dakshineshvar Temple, the great Ramakrishna, with whom I spent heavenly days. The Nayanmars and Alwars held aloft our ancient *dharma* in the Tamil country."

34

THEY walked along the main road, staying in the night at *mandapams*, and finally Shivahari said, "There is Pallamadai, the village where Neelakanta Dikshitar once lived." He told Subbiah about the migration of scholars who once resided in the Vijayanagara Empire to villages around the Thamirabarani River like Pallamadai, Pattamadai, Kodaganallur and Suttamalli, etc. Several scholars resided in these villages and produced works of enduring value. Neelakanta Dikshitar was the nephew of the legendary Advaitic scholar Appaya Dikshitar and was prime minister to King Thirumalai Nayak of Madurai. Dikshitar was one of the foremost Sanskrit scholars of the seventeenth century. He also had the privilege of having a personal vision of Goddess Meenakshi. He contributed to all branches of literature, epic, drama, satire, poetry, and devotional songs. His *Shiva Lilarnavam* is about Lord Shiva in 22 chapters.

There is an interesting story in connection with Neelakanta Dikshitar. Under the instructions of the Pandya king Thirumalai Nayak, the court sculptor carved a statue of the queen. While carving the thigh, his chisel slipped and a mole appeared on it. He made a fresh attempt, discarding the old piece. Again the same mole appeared. This happened five times. When he sought the advice of Dikshitar, who was prime minister, the latter told him, "Go, finish your statue and submit it to the king. The queen actually does have a mole on her thigh." When the statue was presented before the king, he was angry after seeing the mole on the thigh. The sculptor, out of fear, told the king the story. The king wanted to blind the Dikshitar in public. When the soldiers reached him, Dikshitar said, "Go and tell the king that I have already done what he wanted to do." The king, after hearing this, rushed to him and found that Dikshitar had blinded himself with a pair of coals. Realising that Dikshitar was a saint, Thirumalai Nayak presented him with the village Pallamadai. The king then said, "Holy sir, please use your divine powers to get your eyesight back." Neelakanta Dikshitar went to the Meenakshi Temple, composed and sang the poem, *Anandasagarastava*. When he reached the 61st stanza and sang, "with which eyes will I see your lotus feet?" he got his eyesight back.

Shivahari told Subbiah, "Several Dikshits or scholars fled Nasik, on the banks of the Godavari River, when the Muslims attacked the area and forcibly converted people. They went to the courts of the Vijayanagara Empire, the grand Hindu kingdom which revived the glory of Sanatana Dharma and provided sanctuary to many Sanskrit *pandit*s from the north. When the Vijayanagara Empire was attacked by Islamic invaders, many scholars fled further south. Neelakanta Dikshitar was presented with this village Pallamadai and a large number of villages around Tirunelveli near the banks of Thamirabarani. Neelakanta Dikshitar invited his relatives and other families to these villages. The descendants of Swaminatha Dikshitar settled in Melacheval village. Some also went to Kanchipuram. Swaminatha Dikshitar was one such scholar and he was permitted to travel in a palanquin by the Pallava kings of Kanchipuram. Another family settled in a village called Adayapalam and in that blessed fold, the great Advaitic scholar, Appaya Dikshitar was born. Neelakanta Dikshitar was the nephew of Appaya Dikshitar.

"Thus the villages Kodaganallur, Viravanallur, Taruvai, Gopalasamudram, Naranammalpuram, Pattamadai, and Pallamadai were peopled by scholars from Vijayanagara. Pallamadai has a history of enviable scholarship. Swami Dikshitar, the grandson of Appaya Dikshitar, lived here. He wrote *Karttikeya Vijaya*.

35

RAMASUBRAMANIA Dikshitar greeted them at the *agrahaaram*. "Jai Thamirabarani," he said. "Jai Thamirabarani," Shivahari greeted back. Ramasubramanian said, "Revered Sir, it is our privilege to have this great Paramahamsa with us. Please have food with us." "First, let me see the river and the exact spots where Neelakanta Dikshitar did his *upasana*," said Shivahari. They spent a lot of time at the river banks and at the Shiva and Vishnu temple in the village. After lunch, they rested for a while at the house of Ramasubramania Dikshitar. Dikshitar's household was big and his wife fed the guests with the choicest food. "We are proud to have such a great *pandit* among us," she said. Subbiah had sumptuous food after a long time.

"Respected Sir," Dikshitar said in the evening, "There is a great *muni* at Kodaganallur who wants to meet you. His name is Kodaganallur Sundara Swamigal. He has spent several years of penance in the *nanal* bushes (penreed grass) around the Thamirabarani. He gives discourses on *Suta Samhita* and also helps in the restoration of temples in this area. When I met him last I told him that a Paramahamsa who had travelled throughout Bharatavarsha will be staying in our village for a considerable period of time to discourse on great Kashmiri saints. He told me that he wanted to see you." "With pleasure," replied Shivahari. "I also want to come to Kodaganallur. I know the greatness of the village."

They went in a bullock cart arranged by Dikshitar. Subbiah admired the scenic beauty of the area and cool breeze flows from the Podigai Hills. They slept in a *mandapam* and reached Kodaganallur the next day. After bath and ablutions in the river, they had darshan of the presiding deity Brihanmadhava.

At the river side over a deer skin stood Kodaganallur Sundara Swamigal. Shivahari saluted him. Sundara Swamigal was very pleased to learn that Shivahari gained knowledge of the secrets of the Kashmiri saints from his *guru* of the Narmada Valley.

Shivahari's eyes were lit with fire when he thought about the priest of Dakshineshvar. He said to Sundara Swamigal, "I knew a priest at the Dakshineshvar Kali Temple, near Calcutta, the capital city of India. People call him Ramakrishna Paramahamsa. People regard him as an *avatara* of God. He used to say, "*Brahman* is the only reality. The *rishi*s of old attained the Knowledge of *Brahman*." One cannot have this so long as there is the slightest trace of worldliness." How hard the *rishi*s laboured! Early in the morning they would go away from the hermitage, and would spend the whole day in solitude, meditating on *Brahman*. At night they would return to the hermitage and eat a little fruit or roots. They kept their minds aloof from the objects of sight, hearing, touch and other things of a worldly nature. Only thus did they realise *Brahman* as their own inner consciousness. I am privileged to stand before one such sage. I salute you, Sir. My *guru* who lived in the Narmada Valley was also one such. His *guru* lived in Kashmir and initiated him into *brahma-vidya*. My *guru* got some rare palm leaves containing Abhinavagupta's *Tantraloka* and bequeathed them to me. His last wish was that I should bring them out to the world in book form so that humanity benefits from them. He lived with *pandit*s in Kashmir for a long time, learning from them Tantra and Advaita Vedanta. He settled in the Narmada Valley and taught Vedanta to a group of young people including me. A decade has gone after that. I have wandered the length and breadth of Bharatavarsha."

Sundara Swamigal listened to this with rapt attention and said, "I am eager to know about the great Shaivite saints of Kashmir. Can you tell me something about them?"

Shivahari said, "Acharya Abhinavagupta was the foremost scholar in Kashmir Shaivism. He was a brahmin whose ancestors were distinguished scholars in the court of Kanauj. His ancestor was brought by king Lalitaditya to Kashmir, where he was given a big house. Abhinavagupta was a *yoginibhu*, he was born of a *yogini*. His family consisted of members totally devoted to Lord Shiva. Vamana Gupta, his uncle, taught him poetics and Narasimha Gupta, his father, taught him Sanskrit logic and literature. He travelled outside Kashmir to study Shastras under different *acharya*s, including Buddhist and Jain *muni*s. However he owed a lot to Acharya Shambhu Natha from Jalandhara. Gradually Abhinavagupta rose to the position of *acharya*. His *magnum opus* was *Tantraloka* (The Light of the Tantras). He also wrote *Paratrimshika Vivarana, Paramarthasara, Tantrasara* and *Gitartha Samgraha* (*bhashya* on the *Bhagavad-Gita*). He was a master of rhetoric and wrote a *bhashya* on Bharata's *Natya-Shastra* (*Abhinavabharati*) and displayed his mastery over poetics with his *bhashya* on Anandavardhana's *Dhvanyaloka*. Hence Abhinavagupta was truly a multi-faceted personality who exhibited his intellectual prowess in diverse fields. He wrote, "We can free ourselves from *duhkha* by seeing Him (Shiva) in everything, and everywhere. There is no need to renounce the world."

Sundara Swami liked this information on the Kashmiri saints, "Can you tell me something on *Tantraloka*?" he said.

Shivahari said, "Abhinavagupta was an *avatara* of Bhairava Himself. Can I have the privilege of expounding the wealth of Kashmiri Shaivism for the scholars here in front of a *mahatma* like you?"

"You can. I will make the arrangements," the Swamigal replied.

Soon a pandal was erected in the *agrahaaram* and scholars assembled eagerly to listen to "Paramahamsa Shivahari" as they called him. Subbiah was seated near Shivahari. The Swamigal was seated on a tiger skin. Shivahari addressed them.

"Scholars of Kodaganallur, I am a *shishya* of an eminent Acharya from the Narmada Valley. He bequeathed to me manuscripts containing the works of the great saints of Kashmir. It was Lord Shiva Himself who gave this knowledge of the Tantras to the world. Durvasa Rishi meditated in the caves of the beautiful valley of Kashmir and Shiva revealed to him the philosophy of the *abheda* (without differentiation), *Bhairava Tantras*, *bheda-abheda* (with and without differentation) and *bheda* (differentiated). The *rishi* created three sons and initiated the first son, Tryambaka, into the *abheda* doctrine. The word *anuttara* is Shiva and Shakti the supreme consciousness (*cit*), light (*prakasha*), supreme object (*aham*) and eternal vibrations (*spanda*). *Anuttara* is the substratum beneath the universe. It is the unsurpassed reality. It is not different from the universe and the saint who has realised *anuttara* is enlightened and attains perfect freedom (*svatantrya*).

"*Aham* is the interior space of Shiva, the Shakti. *Kaula* is a series of practices which leads to the ascent of consciousness and all the aspects of one's being become a group or a *kula*, supported by Shiva.

"I learnt that all the Smarta scholars here are studying Acharya Sankara's works. Kashmir saints also preach Absolute Monism, the One becoming many but all are one. The one here is the supreme consciousness, Shiva. *Avidya* makes one ignorant of this Shakti. *Svatantrya*, the power of Shiva, enables one to realise one's true identity as Shiva Himself. *Svatantrya* or the power of Shiva grants *shaktipat* or grace. We can remove the *upadhis* or adjuncts that cloud our consciousness only through divine grace for which absolute surrender is required. Tomorrow I will continue my discourse."

The group prostrated before the Swamigal and

Paramahamsa and left. Shivahari and Subbiah stayed at the cattleshed near the temple. Chants from the *Vedapathashala* resonated everywhere. The next day, the group assembled again. Sundara Swamigal was also there. Shivahari continued: "Lord Shiva appeared in the dream of Vasugupta and said, "Go to the Mahadeva Mountain (in Kashmir)." Vasugupta went there and found the *Shiva-Sutra*s inscribed on a rock. The *Shiva-Sutra*s form the Shaiva Monism of Kashmir. They are also known as *Shiva Upanishad Samgraha.*

"The philosophical tradition of Kashmir is known as Trika as it contains the signs, Shiva, his Shakti and *jiva*. It also denotes three primary energies: *para* (supreme) *para-para* (combination of the highest and the lowest) and *apara* (lowest). They are also called *iccha shakti* (energy of will), *jnana shakti* (energy of knowledge) and *kriya shakti* (energy of action). The three energies represent the knower, knowing and known. The Trika *parampara* contains the following systems: *pratyabhijna, kula, krama* and the *spanda.*

"The goal of the Kashmiri Shaivite saints is to lead the *jiva* from individual consciousness to God Consciousness (Parama Shiva). Truth is *anirvachaniya,* unspeakable. The Ultimate Truth can only be experienced. This is self-realisation. Lord Shiva is the source of everything. There is only one being, Shiva. The world is the energy of Shakti. The world of names and differences is the expansion of Shakti — Shiva's energy. Shiva is the Shaktiman (energy holder). The whole objective universe, which includes *pramatri,* the one observing, the subject, *pramana,* the modalities of knowledge, *prameya,* the known object is Shakti.

"Shiva is the ultimate reality from which this universe has emerged and will dissolve into. Shiva and Shakti are like fire and its heat; there is no awareness of separation between the two. This universe is as real as Shiva. He Himself has become everything. This universe is created in the same way as that of the image of an object reflected in a mirror. This theory of reflection is called *Pratibimbavada*. It is Shiva consciousness which is reflected everywhere. Only Shiva consciousness exists. The mirror of Shiva consciousness is the only reality. This reflection is due to *svatantrya* or the independent will of God. This universe is created by Lord Shiva in the mirror of His awareness by this *svatantrya* or independent will. The universe is the expansion of Shiva's Shakti. It is the manifestation of life's nature. Now I think the time has come for your *sandhya* prayers. We shall meet tomorrow."

Shivahari and Subbiah went to the river and while the lad did his *sandhya*, the Paramahamsa meditated on a rock. He chanted verses in praise of Shakti; and suddently went into *nirvikalpa samadhi*. After a long time, he came back to the *sahaja* state and was ecstatic. *Advaitam satyam, advaitam satyam* (Advaita alone is true) — he proclaimed. Subbiah also became joyous and the effulgence of the *atman* shone in their faces. Subbiah recited the *Vivekachudamani*:

> I am neither the doer nor the one who makes others do; I am neither the enjoyer nor one who makes others enjoy; I am neither the seer nor the one who makes others see. I am the self-effulgent *atman* indescribable by qualities.
>
> I am that *Brahman* itself, which is without a second, which is the support of all, which illumines all objects, which has all forms, which is omnipresent, which has no modifications, eternal, pure, without parts, changeless.

He also chanted from the *Atmabodha*:

> *Atman*, which is the sun of knowledge, arises in the firmament of the heart and destroys the darkness. The pervader of all and the sustainer of all, it illumines all and also itself.

Shivahari patted Subbiah on the back and recited from the *Vivekachudamani*:

> All modifications of clay, such as the jar, which are always accepted by the mind as real are (in reality) nothing but clay. Similarly, this entire universe which is produced from the real *Brahman* is *Brahman* itself and nothing but that. Because there is nothing else whatever but *Brahman*, and there is the only self-existent Reality, our very self, therefore art thou that serene, pure, supreme *Brahman*, the One without a second.
>
> That which though one only, is the cause of the many. That *Brahman* art thou. . . .

Shivahari hugged Subbiah and said, "You are a true *shishya*. You have persevered for so long. Perhaps sometimes you think of your father?" "Only sometimes," replied Subbiah, "in fact, rarely. That life is over. I have gained the bliss of the *atman*, due to my relationship with you."

Shivahari said, "Always be careful. Acharya Sankara says:

> If the mind ever so slightly strays from the ideal and becomes outgoing there it goes down and down just as a play ball inadvertently dropped on the staircase bounces down from one step to another.
>
> So be vigilant all the time, Subbiah.

"Gurudeva, can you tell me something about the experience of *samadhi* you had a few minutes ago?" Subbiah asked.

"The Paramahamsa of the Kali temple used to say that in *samadhi* one attains the knowledge of *Brahman*, one realises *Brahman*. In that state reasoning stops altogether, and man becomes mute. He has no power to describe the nature of *Brahman*. He illustrated this with an example. Once a salt doll went to measure the depth of the ocean. It wanted to tell others how deep the water was. But this it could never do, for no sooner did it get into the water than it got dissolved. Now who was there to report about the ocean's depth?" Shivahari said, "A *jivanmukta* is beyond *maya*. As the *Gita* describes him:

> His mind being harmonised by *yoga*, he sees himself in all beings and all beings in himself, he sees the same in all.

"Acharya Sankara says:

> Sometimes a fool, sometimes a sage, sometimes possessed of regal splendour; sometimes wandering, sometimes behaving like a motionless python, sometimes wearing a benignant expression; sometimes honoured, sometimes insulted, sometimes unknown, thus lives the man of realisation, ever happy with Supreme Bliss.

"He further says:

> Though without riches, yet ever content; though helpless, yet very powerful; though not enjoying the sense objects, yet eternally satisfied; though without an exemplar, yet looking upon all with an eye of equality.

"A *jivanmukta* has no identification with his body:

> In reality however, he rests discarding the body, like the snake its slough; and the body is moved hither and thither by the force of the *prana* just as it listeth.

"Such a sage willingly discards his body:

> If a leaf falls in a small stream, or a river, or a place consecrated to Shiva, or in a crossing of roads, of what good or evil effect is that to the tree?
>
> As milk poured into milk, oil into oil, water into water, becomes united and one with it, so the sage who has realised the *atman* becomes one in the *Atman*."

The next day the group of *pandit*s and students assembled at Smarta Street. Several people from Pallamadai, Suttamalli, Melacheval, Gopalasamudram and Pattamadai came to listen to the discourse by the Paramahamsa at Kodaganallur.

"Why did Lord Shiva," continued Shivahari, after giving a brief summary of what he had said the previous day, "create this external objective world? The only reason could be the possibility to recognise his own nature. This objective universe, according to Acharya Abhinavagupta, the greatest philosopher from Kashmir and an *avatara* of Lord Shiva, is the manifestation of Lord Shiva's *svatantra shakti*: It is a tool to realise the universal reality of Shiva. Acharya Abhinavagupta states, "When Lord Shiva is completely alone, bereft of His creation, He exists in the full splendour of His Shiva consciousness. He does not need to recognise it because it is already there, there is nothing to recognise. So, in order to recognise His nature, Shiva must become ignorant of His nature. At least seemingly, He must separate Himself from His nature so that He can experience the joy of recognising it.

"The Universe is the *lila* (play) of Shiva. His *svatantrya* has made him create the universe and he derives joy from recognising his own consciousness. Shiva withdraws from Shiva consciousness and later discovers himself by expanding his consciousness. The universe is the dance of Shiva. The universe has been created by Shiva for him to lose himself and then find himself. *Nimesha* is the withdrawal of Shiva's consciousness and *unmesha* is the expansion of Shiva's consciousness. All these states take place within Shiva. Shiva's seeming loss of His own consciousness and His regaining it is the secret behind the universe and all its activities. We are essentially Parabhairavas, the *avatara*s of Shiva. It is our misfortune that we do not realise it. Then again, in the process of evolution we will realise it. The entire process is impersonal and purely the divine play of Shiva."

An old woman provided buttermilk to the people present. The zamindar of the area too arrived and prostrated before the Paramahamsa.

"Shiva hides Himself," continued Shivahari, "in the particularity of this world with his *maya* created by his *svatantrya shakti* (absolute freedom). This *maya* or *ajnanam* (ignorance) veils the Shiva consciousness. The *Shiva-Sutras* state: "Awareness is the reality of everything. Having differentiated knowledge and not having undifferentiated knowledge is bondage." Knowledge is always present in our conscious self but it is limited, non-full. Real knowledge is knowledge of the self. It is undifferentiated (*nirvikalpa*) and, you are in Parabhairava state. You are Shiva."

The zamindar rose and asked "*Acharya*, how do we become Shiva?"

"You are already Shiva," replied Shivahari, "But you don't realise it. The Shaivite saints of Kashmir have given us three paths to enter into the state of Shiva consciousness from our limited consciousness. The highest path is *shambhavopaya*. The second is *shaktopaya*. The inferior and third state is *anavopaya*.

"The greatest philosopher and saint from Kashmir, Acharya Abhinavagupta tells us in his *magnum opus, Tantraloka,* that the aspirant should try the *shambhavopaya* path first. Abhinavagupta defines the three *upaya*s (paths) as follows: *shambhavopaya* is that *upaya* in which the aspirant gains entry (*samavesha*) into Shiva consciousness (supreme consciousness) just by the grace of his master, without adopting any process. In this method there is no contemplation (*dhyana*), *mantra* or any other aid to meditation.

"*Shaktopaya* is defined as that *upaya* where the aspirant achieves mystic entry (*samavesha*) through contemplation of that mental object which cannot be spoken or recited. *Anavopaya* is that *upaya* where mystical entry takes place through concentration on parts of the body (*sthanaprakalpana*), contemplation (*dhyana*), recitation (*varna*), taking the support of the breath (*uccara*) and *mantra*s.

"Though the means are many, the goal is only one: mystical absorption (*samavesha*) in the *sambhava* state, the reality found in *shambhavopaya* (Shiva consciousness). Our essential nature is Shiva consciousness.

"How do we know what path we should choose?" asked a student from the *pathashala*.

"It depends on the strength of the awareness of the perceived. A Kashmiri scholar has written that the strength of awareness means to possess such powers of subjective consciousness that the aspirant's one-pointed subjective awareness is not overshadowed either by objective experience or thoughts. Most of the people live their lives completely in the objective or cognitive worlds. In the experience of the limited subject, the act of perception or thinking typically overshadows the subject, the perceiver, so that one is aware only of thinking cognitive worlds. Although we might say, "I am seeing a pot," the "I" loses prominence and the act of seeing gets importance. What remains is "seeing a pot." The subject is lost in the act of perception. This is because we mistake the world of diversity for the Ultimate Truth and remain ignorant of one's real universal nature. The strength of awareness is developed by concentrating on the self and being only a witness to thoughts and experiences.

"The aim of *shambhavopaya* is to make the Shivayogi attain the *nirvikalpa* state and be in it continuously. It is a state of thoughtless awareness. From this state the entry of the Shivayogi into Shiva consciousness is automatic. It is only by the grace of God (*Shaktipat*) in the form of the *guru* that Shiva is revealed.

"*Shaktopaya* instructs us to concentrate on the gap between the end of one thought or perception and beginning of another. Within that gap shines the universal reality of Shiva, which is the substratum of All Existence.

"The junction (*sandhi*) has to be caught hold of in order to develop great firmness of awareness. The intensity of this awareness would lead to a continuity of unbroken awareness. This *upaya* states that this could also be practised on the *sandhi* between waking state and dreaming state, between the dreaming state and the state of deep sleep. With the grace of the *guru*, the aspirant can use this method to attain mystical absorption.

"*Anavopaya* asks us to concentrate on breathing, meditative contemplation, experience through a particular sense organ (*karana*), and concentration on some particular place (*sthanaprakalpana*).

"The *yogi* experiences the world immersed with the oneness of God. He experiences God consciousness in whatever he sees and is in a state of mystical trance whether he looks within or without. This leads to a state of *jagadananda* (universal bliss). About this state Abhinavagupta states: "My Master Shambhunatha described *jagad-ananda* as the state that is completely unencumbered, where bliss (*ananda*) is found shining, where it is universally strengthened by the supreme I-consciousness of God, and where the six limbs of *yoga* — *bhavana, dharana, dhyana, pratyahara, yoga* and *samadhi* — are no longer used or required." He becomes a *jivanmukta*. He is Shiva.

"Acharya Abhinavagupta's *bhashya* (commentary) on *Pratyabhijna-Shastra* is as famous as Acharya Sankara's *Bhashya* on *Brahma-Sutras*. Abhinavagupta has written *Bhashya* on *Vimarshini* of Somananda and *Pratyabhijnakarika* of Utpaladeva. *Pratyabhijna* means, to recognise, to realise your self, spontaneously, once again. There are no *upaya*s (means) in the *Pratyabhijna* system. You must simply recognise who you are. The *Pratyabhijna* philosophy is about the *atman* in man and how he is ignorant about it. It exhorts man to realise his divine inheritance and connects him with the one objective reality (Parama Shiva). By removing the veil of ignorance within us and diving deep within we can realise the self — the spark of the divine. Our essential nature is divine. Seeing the self within and understanding that the same self exists with everyone and everywhere will lead to bliss. It is *sarva shivatva*; each individual is Shiva and this knowledge would lead to the understanding of *sarva-samata* (all are born equal), *sarva-svatantrya* (all are born free) and the goal of this philosophy is *vishva-shanti* (peace and tranquillity in the world).

"When Acharya Abhinavagupta felt that he had completed his mission in life, he went to the Bhairava cave in the Himalayas, along with his disciples. He recited the *Bhairava Stotra* which he had himself composed. Leaving his disciples behind, the Acharya entered the Bhairava cave. He never returned.

"My *guru* went to Kashmir and stayed in the Sharada Peeth in the Neelam Valley to study Acharya Abhinavagupta, who was called "Mahamaheshvara." Abhinavagupta wrote *bhashya*s on *Bhagavad-Gita*, Anandavardhana's *Dhvanyaloka* and Bharata's *Natya-Shastra*. Mammata, the author of *Kavya-Prakasha*, refers to him as Abhinavagupta Pada and Sankaracharya of Kashmir. His *Tantraloka* is a masterpiece on Kashmiri Shaivism. He was the very incarnation of Bhairava.

"My *guru* told me tales of Sharada Peeth and other places of learning in Kashmir. He called it the abode of the gods. Every brahmin in south India recites the *Sharada Stotram* — *namaste sharada devi kashmira puravasini*. It is a salutation to Sharada Devi, the Goddess of Learning who resides in Kashmir, the abode of learning in Bharatavarsha. It was the place where Shiva told Parvati about the *amarakatha* — the secret of immortality. My *guru* saw Shiva everywhere in Kashmir and attained supreme Shiva consciousness there. He meditated for two months at the Sankaracharya Temple and Shiva appeared before him, giving divine *darshan*.

"My *guru* told me about the glory of Bharatavarsha. Takshashila was the centre of a great intellectual and spiritual renaissance, which attracted scholars from all over the world. Since Kashmir was not far away from Takshashila the flowering of knowledge spread there. Panini, the author of *Ashtadhyayi*, taught at the University of Takshashila and Patanjali, who was from Kashmir, wrote a famous *Bhashya* on it. Panini was from Pushkalavati, the capital of Gandhara. Panini was one of the greatest intellectuals the world has ever produced. During the reign of king Lalitaditya, Kashmir saw the efflorescence of scholars and spiritual thinkers. Pandit Kalhana, in his *Rajatarangini* has described the history of Kashmir, and its great tradition. My *guru* met *pandit*s and *jivanmukta*s in Kashmir and became a full-fledged practitioner of Vedanta there. He became immersed in the *atman* in the abode of Sharada Devi. The Divine Mother showed him the real nature of man — *Brahman*.

"He told me again and again that the same *atman* resides in the heart of everyone. A strong belief in the supremacy of the self can integrate entire humanity. The One self without a second is seen in the different forms that exist temporarily. The self alone is eternal and has no birth, death and is beyond everything. Abide in the self. The self is the one witness throughout the universe.

"Acharya Sankara's achievements influenced my *guru* a lot. Sri Sankara travelled throughout Bharatavarsha and established maths in the four corners of the country. He conceived of Bharatavarsha as one cultural and spiritual unit from the Himalaya to Kanyakumari and Kamarupa (Assam) to Gandhara (Afghanistan). During his *digvijaya yatra*, he reformed Kapalikas (cannibals with skulls displayed around their neck) who indulged in *bali* worship and unified the different religious sects who exclusively worshipped Shiva, Vishnu, Shakti, Surya, Ganesha and Subrahmanya. The Acharya gave them the unifying vision of Advaita Vedanta, in which *Nirguna Brahman* is manifested in various forms of *saguna* and the many lead only to the One. He crossed the desert and went to Sindhu

Sangama and Purushapura (Peshawar) the captal of Gandhara. At Kashmira (as Kashmir was called in ancient India) he went to the Sharada Peeth which was known as the seat of the highest learning. Acharya Sankara attained *sarvajna pithah* at Sharada Peeth. The Peeth had a door in each corner and the scholar who won the debates entered the door from the corner of Bharatavarsha he represented. The southern wall was never opened since none from the south had, until then, defeated the scholars there. There Acharya Sankara climbed the steps of the temple, each one signifying a particular branch of learning. At each step *pandit*s challenged him in discussion on Nyaya, Vaisheshika, Samkhya, Yoga, Jaina, Buddhist and Mimamsa. He defeated everyone in arguments. The Acharya had mastered all the arts. Each step at the Sharada Temple represents some branch of knowledge and while climbing each step the Acharya answered questions concerning different branches of knowledge asked by experts. A cobbler asked whether the Acharya knew how to stitch *chappal*s. The Acharya took the cobbler's needle and rubbed it against his nose before starting to stitch. This action is typical of a cobbler, and is done to grease the needle with the oily substance found on the sides of the nose so that the needle can penetrate the leather easily. The cobbler was taken by surprise by this and acknowledged that the Acharya knew the trade. The Acharya was the first scholar to enter the southern door.

"Bharatavarsha has seen great saints. One such great soul is Sundara Swamigal who is with us here. I bow to him before taking leave of this sacred village. I appeal to this august gathering which has listened patiently to my discourse to continue to serve our Sanatana Dharma," said Shivahari. He left Kodaganallur for Madurai with Subbiah.

36

SHIVAHARI and Subbiah walked through the tree-shaded road to Madurai. They rested on *mandapams* on the way, taking food from *dharmashalas*. The Paramahamsa became excited when they saw the towers of the Meenakshi Temple overshadowing the city of Madurai. They stayed at Rani Mangammal Chatram and partook of food from there.

Shivahari became intoxicated with the hoary past of Madurai and repeated loudly, "Meenakshi, Meenakshi." As they entered the temple, Shivahari saw the idols of the 63 Nayanmars (Shaivite saints) in the temple and tears came from his eyes. Seeing Goddess Meenakshi, he went into *samadhi*. After a while, Subbiah assisted him inside the *sanctum sanctorum*, with the help of the priest. A ray of effulgence passed through the idol, and to the utter disbelief of Subbiah, the Goddess herself appeared before them, beautifully decked and luminous.

"Divine mother, divine mother," said Shivahari.

"You are one of the greatest of *bhaktas*," said the Goddess.

"All due to your grace. I am your slave, mother Meenakshi" he said. "Continue your noble work; spread the philosophy of the Acharya Abhinavagupta and Acharya Sankara — they were the *avataras* of Mahadeva himself," the Goddess said.

"Divine Mother, I don't know whether I deserve this honour. This is my *shishya* Subbiah. We both will undertake this task," said an overwhelmed Shivahari.

Goddess Meenakshi came near them, touched their hands and dissappeared. Shivahari, Subbiah and the priest were in a trance.

Outside the temple Shivahari said, "We shall finish our pilgrimage to Rameshwaram and then do the task given to us by the Divine Mother, Meenakshi."

37

Reaching Tiruchuli, they rested in a big *chatram* (choultry) there. Shivahari told Subbiah that the town was named Tiruchuli because Lord Shiva made circular holes (*chuzhi*) in the land when the whole world was submerged during the great deluge (*pralaya*). Thus Shiva saved this place. Bhuminatha and Sri Sahayavalli preside over the town. Appar, Sundarar, Manikkavacakar and Sambandar have written exquisite songs in the temple in praise of the Lord and His consort. Near the temple flows quietly the sacred river Kaundinya, named after sage Kaundinya. The sage had done *tapasya* here and as a boon Shiva brought the Ganga in the form of the Kaundinya to this place. The temple tank is called Trishulatirtham, as it was created by Shiva with his *trishula* (weapon). Goddess Ganga bathes in this tank every year on the full moon day of the month of Masi (February-March) and worships Lord Shiva here. During the waxing fortnight of the moon, just prior to the full moon, the water in the tank rises gradually reaching the maximum on the full moon day, after which it decreases gradually during the waning fortnight, to reach its previous level on the succeeding new-moon day.

A few pilgrims in the *chatram* prostrated before the Paramahamsa. "O! Wise sage, bless us," they said, "Please be our teacher."

Paramahamsa Shivahari said, "Yadu who knew the Shastras saw a wise young *avadhuta* moving about fearlessly. He said: "O brahmin you are indeed free from ego. Please tell me how you attained this wisdom which enables you to roam, free from care like a child, everywhere. Usually men seek religion and desire knowledge with the ulterior motive of gaining success, fame and prosperity. But you, who are shrewd, talented, learned, a good speaker, capable of achieving success, does not work or make the least exertion for your own good! It is as if you are an idiot. And yet while people are being scorched by the strong fire of lust and greed, you remain untouched by its heat. O brahmin, please tell me how you, though living a solitary life find delight in thy self alone, untouched by the miseries of the world.

"The noble brahmin replied, "I roam on earth a free soul, having received wisdom from many teachers. Listen and hear who are my teachers: the earth, air, ether, water, fire, the moon, the sun, the pigeon, the python, the sea, the moth, the elephant, the bee, the honey gatherer, the deer, the fish, the courtesan, *pingala*, the osprey, the child, the maiden, the arrow-maker, the snake, the spider and a particular insect known as *bhramara kita*. These are the 24 teachers from whom I have gathered my wisdom."

"As the spider weaves its thread," Shivahari continued, "out of its own mouth, plays with it and then withdraws it again into itself, so the eternal, unchangeable Lord, who is formless and attributeless, who is absolute knowledge, and absolute bliss evolves the whole universe out of Himself, plays with it, and again withdraws it into Himself.

"The *atman* alone IS, one without a second. The *atman* alone is reality. Learn to see the One in the many. The *atman* is separate from the body, the mind, the intellect. He is the eternal witness.

"The *Taittiriya Upanishad* states:

> The knower of *Brahman* attains the supreme; it has been proclaimed like this: *Brahman* is Truth, consciousness, and infinity; one who knows this truth, hidden in the supreme cavity of the heart enjoys all desires along with the all-knowing *Brahman*.

"The *Brihadaranyaka Upanishad* in its dialogue between Yajnavalkya and Maitreyi depicts the immortal, infinite and non-dual *atman* as the *antaryami*, inner self:

> The *atman*, O Maitreyi, is to be realised, is to be heard about, and meditated upon; when the *atman* is realised, heard about, thought about, and known, this whole manifested universe becomes known.

A large group of pilgrims gathered outside the *chatram* to listen to Paramahamsa Shivahari. Shivahari was in a state of superconsciousness and words of the ancient Upanishadic *rishi*s poured out from his lips. People listened with rapt attention. Subbiah sat proudly next to him. Subbiah said, "The Paramahamsa of Kali temple, Dakshineshvar, Bengal, said, that one ultimately discovers god by trying to know who this "I" is. Is this "I" the flesh, the bones, the blood, or the marrow? It is the mind or the *buddhi*? Analysing thus you realise that you are none of these. This is called the process of *neti, neti*, not this, not this." The spiritual aspirant has six spiritual treasures — control of the mind, control of the senses, tranquillity, endurance, concentration and potential faith. As gold, purified by thorough heating on the fire gives up its impurities and attains to its own brilliance, so the mind through meditation gives up the impurities and attains the reality of *Brahman*."

News spread around about the Paramahamsa and a crowd gathered around the *chatram*. *Pandit*s from the *agrahaaram* invited him to the house of Sundaram Iyer, a stamp vendor and uncertified pleader. Shivahari and Subbiah were given sumptuous food by Sundaram Iyer who was extremely hospitable. "I feel some vibrations here," proclaimed Shivahari. "I feel that Shiva himself would be born in this town as an *avatara* soon. Concentrate on *abhyudaya* (welfare in social and economic fields) as well as *nihshreyasa* (inward spiritual journey). Acharya Sankara says in his *Gita-Bhashya* that twofold is the philosophy taught in the Vedas. One is the philosophy of *pravritti*, action, the other is the philosophy of *nivritti*, withdrawal from action, that is meditation. Both are needed to establish a stable world order. These days Vedic studies are dying and many brahmins are moving to secular jobs. But never give up the Upanishads. That is the great strength of Bharatavarsha."

38

A GROUP of pilgrims who were travelling to Manamadurai accompanied Shivahari and Subbiah. On the way while they rested in *mandapams* the Paramahamsa told them the story of Acharya Sankara.

Acharya Sankara, as an eight years old *brahmachari*, went in search of Acharya Govindapada who lived in a cave on the banks of the river Narmada. He did his prayers every day and sought *bhiksha* in the houses on the way. Sankara entered the cave where Govindapada was meditating and sang a hymn *Dasa-shloki* which began with the lines, "I am not earth, nor water, nor fire, nor air, nor space, nor a combination of all these which are with the realm of change, but the one changeless Shiva am I. . . ." Govindapada opened his eyes and was pleased to accept Sankara as his *shishya*. He agreed to impart *brahma-vidya* to Sankara. When the Narmada was in flood, the waters threatened to enter the cave where Govindapada was meditating. Sankara took his *kamandalu* and placed it at the entrance of the cave. As the waters touched its mouth it receded and the river was normal. Govindapada, when he learnt this feat of Sankara, blessed the monk with the following words, "Just as you contained the flood waters in your *kamandalu*, you should write commentaries on the Shastras condensing in them the essence of all the Vedas. By this work you will gain eternal glory."

Acharya Sankara's first work was his commentary on *Vishnu Sahasranama*. He went to Kashi and lived at Manikarnika Ghat near the Vishvanatha Temple and propounded the doctrine, "*Brahman* is the only Reality." At Badarikashrama, the Acharya finished his *bhashyas* on the *Brahma-Sutras*, twelve

Upanishads, and *Bhagavad-Gita* (the three together are called *Prasthanatrayi*). He also taught *brahma-vidya* to the people there, including the king himself."

39

THE group reached Manamadurai and the news of the arrival of the saint reached the *agrahaaram* there. Shivahari took Subbiah to the *samadhi* of Sadashiva Brahmendra which was in the town. Shivahari said, "He was a prodigy by birth and his father was a great *pandit*, Moksha Somasundara Avadhani. His original name was Shivaramakrishnan. He was persuaded by his parents to marry and after the attainment of maturity by his wife, the first night was arranged in his in-law's house. He was extremely hungry that night and requested his mother-in-law to give him a little food. She said "Oh! Just wait. You don't have to wait too long. Don't step in, stand there." Shivaramakrishnan saw a philosophical meaning in these words and considered the words "don't step in" by his mother-in-law as conveying a message from God that he should not step into *grihastha ashrama*. He left the house without the knowledge of anyone. He became a preceptor of Advaita, seeing *Brahman* everywhere. He was an Avadhuta who wandered semi-naked in a state of Brahmic bliss and composed the great Advaitic text, *Atma-Vidya-Vilasa*. He also composed a series of musical compositions in praise of Sri Rama and Sri Krishna. His poetic signature was "Paramahamsa." He also wrote a lot of philosophical works such as *Brahma-Sutra-Vritti, Yoga Sudhakara, Kaivalya Amrita Bindu* (on Upanishad) *Siddhanta Kalpavalli* (a poetic treatise on Appaya Dikshitar's works), *Advaita Rasa Manjari* and others. His masterpiece is *Atma-Vidya-Vilasa* which runs into 62 verses and deals with renunciation. An Avadhuta is one who has realised the self and is immersed in the bliss of *Brahman*. Such a person has gone beyond the Veda and the Shastra:

Discard the bondages of *karma*. Wander in the hills immersed

> in the bliss of the self-unmindful of the world like a deaf and blind man.
>
> Rooted in the *Brahman* absorbed in the bliss within, he for a while meditates, sings and dances in ecstasy.
>
> He sees nothing, hears nothing. He is immersed, in *Brahman* and in that intoxication is motionless."

While quoting these verses, Shivahari went into *nirvikalpa samadhi* and was in the state for four hours.

While walking along the Vaigai River in Manamadurai, Shivahari said to Subbiah, "We should transfer our mind to the whole world, as if the whole world is thinking. Never think that you are someone belonging to a particular place, but think like the whole world thinking. The world is a big organism like our body. It is beyond caste; beyond philosophy. A *paramahamsa* goes beyond the four *ashramas*. The ancient *rishis* contemplated the cosmos as a unitary structure and visualised the human being as an inseparable part of the cosmos. The Upanishads tell us that we are neither men nor women. We are eddies, waves in the ocean of cosmic power. Once we understand that we are the *atman* and the *atman* is nothing but *Brahman* we can get serenity. People who have lost the consciousness of the self are killers of the self according to *Ishavasya Upanishad*. The universe of names and forms is nothing but the self and the *jnani* is like the goldsmith who sees ornaments as various aspects of gold. Acharya Sankara used his genius to evolve a consistent system out of the diverse declarations of the Upanishads. Using the tools of *tarka* (discussion), *anubhava* (experience), *yukti* (reason) and *shruti* (revelation) he brought out to the world the philosophy of the *atman*. The Ultimate Truth is transcendental; god is beyond space, time and causation. Only *aparoksha anubhava* or immediate experience can reveal the truth of the Absolute. There is no perceiver or perceived. In the Upanishads, man does not conceive of God, but God knows that He is. "I am" is the knowledge of God. There is a difference between the knowledge of God and the knowledge of man. Man's knowledge can be stated as: "I am and others also are." But God's knowledge consists of "I am and nothing else exists" This "I" includes everything and there is no space, time, causation. It is a state of pure consciousness.

"Yajnavalkya tells Maitreyi, "Nothing is dear for its own sake; for the sake of the *atman*, everything is dear. When we love a thing, we love our *atman*. The *atman* is hidden in all things of the world. It is the Supreme Self that is pulling the supreme self." This is the great statement of *Brihadaranyaka Upanishad*. Consciousness, the self, is the universal perceiver. The Upanishad states, "you will see another only when there is duality" Consciousness is the only reality. What does God see? He sees Himself only. Again the Upanishad states; "Who will know the knower? Who will think of the thinker? Who will understand the understander? Who will be conscious of consciousness? It knows all things because it alone is everywhere. It does not know anything because outside it, nothing is. God does not know anything because outside Him nothing is; but God knows everything because he Himself is everything. The same Upanishad states, "There is no gulf between the seer and the seen. Therefore the seer alone reigns supreme." The sole seer is the sea of consciousness. The entire sea of consciousness, the universe which is all-seeing is aware of itself. It is *Brahma-loka*. Yajnavalkya tells Janaka, "O Your Highness! This is *Brahma-loka*, the goal of life. It is the supreme bliss." With a drop of this universe of Bliss the entire creation is sustained. The joys of the world are just one drop of this universal *Brahman* Bliss."

Subbiah listened with great devotion and his determination to be a realised soul grew.

"Bharatavarsha," said Shivahari, "reached its peak in the statement of Yajnavalkya: *idam brahma, idam kshatram, ime lokah, ime devah, imani bhutani, idam sarvam, yad ayam atma* — This source of knowledge, this source of power; all these worlds; all these gods; all these beings; all this is just the self. Subbiah, you are the stars, you are the sky, and you are the space."

As Subbiah slept in the *mandapam* that night, the words, you are stars, you are the sky, and you are the space, kept echoing in his mind.

40

THE group left Manamadurai and travelled through Paramakudi and reached Thirupullani, one of the *divya deshams* in the Vaishnava religion. It was the place where Vibhishana surrendered to Sri Rama. Shivahari told the group about the place. Sri Rama, here, invoked the Samudraraja in order to cross the ocean and reach Lanka. Sri Rama placed blades of *kusha* grass on the sands of the beach at Thirupullani and saluted the sea God by joining his palms. Then he lied down on that bed of *darbham* facing eastward and using his mighty arm as a pillow for his head. This has been beautifully described by Valmiki. Shivahari took out a manuscript from his jute bag and read out the relevant passage from Valmiki. He also quoted from Thirumangai Alwar's description of the scene.

The group walked to Rameshwaram and stayed at Venkataraya *chatram*. "I learnt from a *parivrajaka* that this was where Khudiram Chattopadhyaya, the blessed father of the Paramahamsa of Dakshineshvar Temple near Calcutta stayed. This is indeed a holy spot," Saying so, Shivahari kissed the floor of the *chatram*. He immediately had a vision of an old man standing on the banks of the Indus River, and chanting Vedic hymns in an ancient manner:

> O come, Thou Effulgent One, thou bestower of blessings, Signifier of *Brahman* in three letters! Salutation be to thee, O Gayatri, Mother of Vedic *mantras*, Thou who hast sprung from *Brahman*!

From Shivahari's eyes the pilgrims could see the glow of the Vedic Aryans who communed with the gods. They stayed at Rameshwaram for a month.

Shivahari and Subbiah walked in the evening along the sea-shore.

"Is the world in perfect order, Acharya?" asked Subbiah.

"The *Gita* envisages," Shivahari said, "universal synthesis and the ultimate balance of everything. Human beings are caught in *maya* which consists of *sattva, rajas* and *tamas.* They are tied by ropes of likes and dislikes. They suffer from internal conflicts and caught in a web of relationships, attachments, aversions. These relationships are metaphysically conditioned, cosmically organised by impersonal law which has no friends or foes. Ignorance of this cosmic law leads to mistakes and unhappiness. The ignorant derive joy and grief in the world. The *jnani* is beyond all such emotions as he knows that everything is cosmically oriented. Bhagavan Buddha said that everything is transitory, momentary; everything is a link connecting itself with another link. There is a procession of events. The *Gita* states that you are neither the doer nor the deed. The *atman* within us is the symbol of the Absolute everywhere. The Vedic *rita* or cosmic law ensures balance in the universe. Ensnared by the senses, man forgets his true identity. Life is a *yajna,* sacrifice. We are part of a complex network. The aim of human birth is to perceive the self in us and understand that the same self is there in all beings — *yena sarvam idam tatam* — the self of ours pervades the self of all beings. Desire is the secret behind the sorrow of men. Desires carry the seeds of sorrow with them. Do your alloted duty without caring for the fruits of the labour. Be rooted in the *atman.* You are not the senses, body, mind, intellect. Be a witness to your thoughts. Understand that you are the self. The *Chhandogya Upanishad* states:

> Suppose, good lad, that someone were to lead a man blindfold from Gandhara and then release him in a deserted place; and suppose that he were to be blown to east, north, south or

> west, crying "I have been led blindfold and released blindfolded!"
>
> And suppose that someone were to undo the blindfold and tell him, "Gandhara is in this direction. Walk in this direction." And he, being wise and intelligent, by asking from village to village, would reach Gandhara. In the same way a person who has a teacher knows, "It is only so long until I am released. Then I will reach my goal."
>
> This subtle part is what all this has as self. It is truth; it is the self. You are that, Shvetaketu."

Both of them visited the spots in the area connected with Śri Rama and had *darshan* of Lord Shiva in the temple where Sri Ramachandra prayed to expiate the sin of having killed the brahmin Ravana. Shivahari narrated to the people in the *chatram* stories from Valmiki and Vyasa and infected them with the spirit of *bhakti* and *jnana*. Subbiah admired the exquisite architecture of the Rameshwaram Temple.

41

AFTER returning to Madurai, Shivahari and Subbiah went to the Meenakshi Temple everyday. "O! Meenakshi, O! Meenakshi! Take me in your fold," Shivahari exclaimed. They meditated inside the Pudumantapam (Vasanta Mandapam) near the temple, under the care of statues of *yali*s of Vijayanagara fame and the grand Thirumalai Nayakar with his wives, welcoming people. Shiva, with his 64 visages, stared at them. The Vasanta Mandapam surrounded by a watercourse, was the summer retreat of the Gods. Shivahari narrated stories from the *Tiru Vilayadal Puranam* to the pilgrims who flocked to Vasanta Mandapam, acting out the scenes of the Lord's *lila*. At the *siddhar* shrine in the temple, where Shiva appeared to the king in the guise of a Siddhar, Shivahari went into *samadhi*. "Here is Dakshinamurty himself in human form," thought Subbiah. At the Velliambalam, the shrine of Nataraja, Shivahari appeared as the cosmic dancer to Subbiah, exulting in Ananda Tandavam. Shivahari narrated to him the dance between Kali and Oordhva Thandavar (Shiva). The statue of Thayumanavar fascinated them since it symbolised the rescue act of the Lord for a woman in the delivery of her child when river Cauvery (Kaveri) was flooded. Thayumanavar, He is also a mother. Indeed He is everything, Subbiah thought. Another statue of the Lord as a coolie and the king beating him with a cane was prominent. The frescoes depicting the *lila* of the Lord (*Tiruvilayadal*) enthralled Subbiah who knew that the entire universe is nothing but the play of God. Statues of Kala Samharar, Pashupata Moorthy, Uma Maheshvarar, Chandrasekarar, Rishaba, Suhasanar, Somaskandhar, Bikshadanar, Veera Bhadrar, Kratha Arjuna, Gaja Samharar and a host of others kept the lad in a spiritually uplifted mood. The Paramahamsa stopped in front of each statue and narrated stories from the Puranas or *Mahabharata* in connection with it.

The statue of Ardhanarishvara, reminded him that Shiva is nothing without Shakti and the latter is his acting power. The one dealing with Kalyana Sundareshvarar was about the Divine marriage between Parvati as Meenakshi, who was the daughter of the Pandya king to Shiva. Myth after myth reminded him of the glory of the Lord and the divinity pervading everywhere. The statue of Chakradhanar was of special interest. Vishnu prayed to Shiva in order to defeat a *rishi* and the mischievous Lord stole one lotus flower from the prayer collection of 1000 lotus flowers. Subsequently, when the 1000th *mantra* came, the relevant flower was absent. Vishnu quickly plucked one of his eyes, thinking he had made a mistake. Shiva appeared before him and restored his eyes, hailing him as Kamala Kannan or the Lotus-eyed and also gifted him a disc to defeat enemies. The Mukkuruni Pillaiyar gave a benign look at Subbiah. At the Killikootu Mandapam the five Pandava brothers with their bows (Bhima of course with his mace) welcomed them. The swing hall or the Oonjal Mandapam is the place where Meenakshi and Sundareshvarar are exhibited on Fridays on swings gently swayed by the priests. The frescoe displaying Bikshadanar who wanted to chastise the lazy *rishi*s of Tharuga Vana and asked Vishnu to come in the guise of Mohini was explained in detail by Shivahari.

Shivahari and Subbiah walked to the ship-shaped Thenur Mandapam on the Vaigai River near Vandiyur. They meditated inside it while brahmin boys with tufts were seated in a row on the opposite side performing their *sandhya* prayers. The Nayak kings once witnessed the entry of Lord Kallazhagar into Vaigai which took place at Thenur village. The Paramahamsa took out from his jute bag old poem leaves containing Dattatreya's *Avadhuta Gita* and read them aloud:

> When the pot is broken, the space within it is absorbed in the infinite space and becomes undifferentiated. When the mind becomes pure, I do not perceive any difference between the mind and the Supreme Being.
>
> Know me to be that self who is everything and everywhere at all times, who is eternal, steady, the all, the non-existent, and the existent.
>
> There are no Vedas, no worlds, no gods, no sacrifices. There is certainly no caste, no stage in life, no family, no birth. There is neither the path of smoke nor the path of light. There is only the highest truth, the homogeneous *Brahman*.
>
> There is no body made up of five elements; nor is there anyone who is disembodied. All is verily the self alone. How can there be the three states and the fourth?
>
> I am not the doer or enjoyer. Work have I none, now or formerly. I have no body, nor am I bodiless. How can I have or not have a sense of "my-ness?"
>
> Giving up the body in a holy place or in the house of a *chandala*, the *yogi*, even if he has lost consciousness, becomes identified with the Absolute as soon as he is free of the body.

Saying so, the Paramahamsa went into *nirvikalpa samadhi*. The boys had finished their *sandhya* and looked at the sage with curiosity and left for playing marbles on the river bed.

The next day both of them went to the Mariamman Teppakulam; admired the huge temple tank and its ornate architecture. Shivahari pointed to Subbiah two birds on the temple column and quoted the *Mundaka Upanishad*:

> Two birds, companions (who are) always united, cling to the self-same tree. Of these two, the one eats the sweet fruit and the other looks on without eating.
>
> On the self-same tree, a person immersed (in the sorrows of the world) is deluded and grieves on account of his helplessness. When he sees the other, the Lord who is

> worshipped and His greatness, he becomes freed from sorrow.
>
> Sporting in the self, delighting in the self, performing works, such a one is the greatest of the knowers of *Brahman*.

Subbiah was overwhelmed by these verses and he concentrated on the upper bird, the *atman*. He said, *ekameva advitiyam* (one without a second)." He went into *nirvikalpa samadhi*:

> He who knows *Brahman* becomes *Brahman*. Between *Brahman* and the knower of *Brahman* there is not the least difference. There is nothing impossible for such a free soul. There is no more birth and death for him. He is free forever.

When he came back to normalcy, Shivahari hugged him and said, "You will be known hereafter as a Paramahamsa. Your new name is Swami Krishna Chaitanya." Tears of gratitude came from Subbiah's eyes. Shivahari remarked, "Ramakrishna Paramahamsa of Dakshineshvar Temple said, "When one experiences all the states from that of sweepers to that of emperors and is really convinced of their worthlessness, one can be in the state of a real Paramahamsa, a true knower of *Brahman*." A Paramahamsa is a supreme swan. Like the swan which is not affected by the water in the lake, the advaitin is not ensnared by the *maya* of the world."

The next day at the Puthu Mandapam, Shivahari said, "In the *Panchadashi* Vidyaranya gives the example of the light that is kept on the stage of a theatre. The light illumines all actors — kings, servants, etc. — and the audience. The light is there all the time, even when the performance is over. The self gives light to the ego (*ahamkara*), intelligence (*buddhi*), mind (*chitta*) and lower mind without itself being affected. Even during deep sleep when the ego is not felt, the self shines of itself and remains attributeless. Realise the self."

42

THEY went to *Srivilliputhur* and had *darshan* of Lord Vishnu there. Shivahari said, "Krishna Deva Raya, the king of the Vijayanagara Empire, wrote the beautiful Telugu work, *Amuktamalyada,* describing Andal's feeling for her cosmic lover, Lord Vishnu. Though the focus is on Godadevi, the Sanskrit name of Andal, there are sub-stories as well. The king himself came here and was instrumental in the construction of this huge *gopuram.* He patronised Sri Vaishnavism, constructed *mandapams* in the Tamil country, besides maintaining a few temples. When the Islamic invaders were plundering the country, the Vijanayanagara Empire protected Sanatana Dharma."

Shivahari had visions of Andal and her illustrious father Perialvar. He went into *samadhi.* They stayed in a *chatram* and Subbiah read the Upanishads in the evening.

They walked from Srivilliputhur to Madurai. "Appaya Dikshitar," said Shivahari, "finished his studies on the 14 *vidya*s when he was young. Monarchs bowed before him. He contributed a lot to several branches of knowledge and his Shivadvaita is famous. For him everything was the manifestation of *Brahman.* His *Atmarpana-stuti* is on the self. In *Anandalahari Chandrika* he reconciles divergent *darshan*s and proves that the Advaita of Sri Sankara is the eternal truth. He expounded the philosophy of Sri Sankara with missionary zeal in his works. His *Parimala* on Vedanta is a standing testimony to his scholarship. He was an outstanding intellectual and a supreme *yogi.* Other works include *Madhavatantramukha Mardana, Ramanujashringabhanga* and he was, like Acharya Sankara and Acharya Abhinavagupta, an *avatara* of Shiva. The *Nyayamanjari* is on *Brahma-Sutras* and follows Sri Sankara's viewpoint. It is magnificent. It would require volumes to cover the life of this great *yogi*. Someday I hope you will do it."

Shivahari went into a meditative mood and repeated the verses from *Isha Upanishad*.

"The *Isha Upanishad* States:

> He who sees all beings in his very self and the self in all beings — he is not averse to anything. In whom, the wise one, all beings are just the self, then what delusion, what sorrow is there for him, who sees Oneness (everywhere)?"

At Madurai Shivahari continued his discourses and they drew large crowds.

"Acharya Sankara stated," said Shivahari, "that the self exists and it is everywhere. The self knows without knowing anything outside itself. Therefore the self is universal Existence. Acharya stated that the *atman* is *Brahman* and is the all-pervading universality. All our thoughts are manifestations of wholeness. Every thought is total. Acharya Sankara was a metaphysician and a spiritual teacher. He was also a social reformer. He taught us that even an ant or an elephant, you and I are sparks of that cosmic source. We are essentially divine. Acharya Sankara was an integrator. He united different ways of *saguna* worship. He stated that we are all connected by the same *atman*. We are children of immortality. We are potential gods. The existence of self unites everyone."

*Pandit*s admired the insights of this Paramahamsa with matted locks. He seemed to be divinity personified.

Subbiah admired the beautifully carved sculptures of monkeys, snakes, cows, *Shivalinga*s and even turtles inside the *mandapam*. There were Vinayakas and Krishnas everywhere. These *mandapam*s combine the divine with the natural world; the Hindu mind sees the Divine in the smallest ant. Shivahari said: "Our Dharmashastras state that building such rest places for pilgrims is one of the 32 acts of service to humanity. Subbiah, look at that bell. Thirumalai Naicker had a lot of respect for the Andal Temple at Srivilliputhur. He had his lunch only after the noon *puja*. The big bronze bell would toll, as soon as the *puja* was over for 5 km. There are a series of *mandapams* between Srivilliputtur and the palace of Naicker king. The bell would be tolled from one *mandapam* to another and within a few minutes the bell sound is carried to Madurai. Besides, these *mandapams* serve as free rest places for pilgrims. They can survive for centuries and withstand nature's fury. People cook here; look at all the sculptors of kings, rich people including women greeting pilgrims and wayfarers. In Bharatavarsha each soul is seen as potentially divine and kings and wealthy people believed that serving humanity is serving the divine."

Shivahari said, "The great Sankaracharya, in his commentary on the *Brihadaranyaka Upanishad*, states:

> Even before the realisation of *Brahman*, all beings, being one with *Brahman* are always one with all other beings; but, through spiritual ignorance alone comes the (false) notion that one is not *Brahman* and not one with all, just like a mother-of-pearl is mistaken for silver, or the sky is mistaken to be spatially limited or affected by dirt or impurity.

"Sankaracharya further says:

> There is no difference between great, courageous sages like sage Vamadeva, and people of limited energy of the present age, so far as their being *Brahman*, or (their inherent capacity for) its realisation, is concerned.

"The great Sankaracharya in his *Brahma-Sutra-Bhashya* states:

> "Of this universe, which is differentiated by the activities of names and forms, which consists of many actors and enjoyers, which is strictly regulated by the fruits of the action of space, time and causality, which is so vast and complex in its structure as to be beyond even the capacity of thought

> and imagination to comprehend the cause of the origin, maintenance and dissolution of such a universe is possible only from that Reality who is all-knowing and all-powerful that is *Brahman*.

"Sankaracharya was a great missionary of Sanatana Dharma at a time when it was in a decayed state and Buddhism reigned in the country. He went from kingdom to kingdom of Bharatavarsha and established the Sanatana Dharma. Within a short span of 32 years he achieved what would take several births for ordinary people. He was a *yogi*, an eminent author of commentaries, and hymns and an *eka-chanda-grahi* (one who retained what he heard but once). When Padmapada, one of the disciples of Sri Sankara, lost his commentary on his *Brahma-Sutra-Bhashya*, titled *Vijaya Dindima*, the Acharya dictated to him from his memory the complete commentary. King Rajashekhara came to Kalady to meet Sri Sankara who was well known in the area as a child prodigy. The king recited his three plays before the child and later when these works were accidentally destroyed, our Acharya who was precocious, used his retentive memory, and dictated them."

Shivahari and Subbiah travelled to Bhaskararajapuram (near Kumbakonam) where a great saint Bhaskararaya Acharya once lived and returned to Pallamadai. From there, they climbed the Agastya mountains. Shivahari, inside the thick forests, instructed Subbiah on *Brahman*. One day seated in a yogic posture, inside a cave, Shivahari recited the following verses from *Brihadaranyaka Upanishad*:

> The great birthless self is undecaying, immortal, undying, fearless and *Brahman* (infinite). *Brahman* is indeed fearless, He who knows it as such becomes the fearless *Brahman*.

With these words the Paramahamsa got a vision of Goddess Meenakshi and merged with *Brahman*, attaining *samadhi*.

Subbiah preached Sanatana Dharma for 50 years in several places in India and attained *samadhi* in Karachi in the early part of the twentieth century.

43

I LISTEN to the lecture by Professor Ramachandra Gandhi at the university and also interact with him after the session. He is a true *sadhaka* and an expert *par excellence* on non-dual philosophy; in fact, he interprets everything through non-dualism. I learn that he calls out to Ramana Maharshi often, referring to the saint as "apa." He believes that compassion is a natural by-product of non-dualism; you empathise with joy and pain in everyone, seeing the indwelling self in everything. The Professor asks us, "Who am I? Who are we? What is the truth of India? Can the dualism of self and other be dissolved and resolved?" He talks about the Sapta Rishis of Modern India: Ramakrishna Paramahamsa, Vivekananda, Aurobindo, J. Krishnamurti, Ramana Maharshi, Tagore and Mahatma Gandhi. "True sovereignty can only be of the self, limitless self-awareness," he says. In our private talk he hails Ramana Maharshi as the greatest mind-slayer of all time. He soon becomes a *sahridaya* and I admire his use of gestures while speaking. He says that the three R's should be replaced by three E's ethics, ecology and enlightenment. He draws deeply from the *Mahabharata*, the *Bhagavatam* and the *Ramayana* for solutions to modern problems. He feels that the *Mahabharata* contains solutions to modern man's problems and quotes profusely from it. His Advaita-based *ahimsa* makes him preach vegetarianism as an ideal for everyone to adopt. His famous puns (most of India's elections are naturally rigged, because Indian culture follows *Rigveda*) and splendid sense of humour captivate me.

I visit him at the Indian Institute of Culture in Delhi and continue my dialogues with him. Most of the time he talks and he is a compulsive talker. The conversations are never boring and this friendship calms my mind.

But my search continues. I fly to Mumbai and meet Ramesh Balsekar, the Advaita *guru* and disciple of Nishargadatta Maharaj. He says that, "the mystery behind the universe is impersonal consciousness seeking its source. In the evolutionary process of identification, the mind is turned inward and the process of disidentification begins and the true identification begins and the true identity is revealed. It is an impersonal process. The individual organism is only a mechanism through which this process is taking place. Consciousness is the only reality. The individual is only an object. True nature of an individual is consciousness. The seeker begins to get the sense of presence, the sense of I AM. During the waking state the individual has his sense of awareness which is absent in deep sleep. The sense of presence is absent in deep sleep. Existence is based on duality — for example beauty, goodness. Everything is interrelated and cannot exist without the other. Human perception is limited. We should see the universe as totality, there would be no choosing, no unhappiness. The Universe is a whole. The phenomenal world is subject to change and nothing is constant. We keep chasing security. Life is based on opposites. Everything is perfectly arranged. The whole process is impersonal. We are only characters in a play. The phenomenon of life is only impersonal consciousness seeking its source and its true nature through body-mind systems. There is one totality of consciousness. Consciousness becomes aware of itself through I AM. Awareness means duality. "I AM" is absent in deep sleep. Awareness leads to duality which again leads to manifestation. The Existence of the manifestation has to be observed. We are mere three-dimensional objects. Observing takes place through individual body-mind organism through which impersonal consciousness observes its own manifestation. So we have observing, observer and observed.

The observer object assumes subjectivity and hence dualism comes into being. The ME idea comes due to duality. The only subject is the totality of God who observes the individual organism. The observer object assumes subjectivity — Me and other concepts evolve and becomes observer subject and gets separated from rest of universe as God's object. Realisation occurs when the observer subject understands that it is only an object and there is a reversal from dualism. The observer object is not a subject and the only subject is the totality of God. Tension and unhappiness occur when we assume that we are the subject, and inter-human relationships get strained. We are observed objects and merely instruments through which the totality of God happens.

"The idea of seeking is part of the process of evolution; it is consciousness identifying itself. The mind turns inward and realises that there is no real me. It is mere impersonal process of evolution and the body, mind organs are meant for the action to take place. It is impersonal consciousness identifying itself. There is no entity and the process goes on through objects. The disciple and *guru* are part of the process of consciousness identifying itself. The individual is only an object and the true nature is consciousness which works through the body and mind mechanisms. Enlightenment is the process of identification turning inward and the process of disidentification. It is the perennial philosophy, involving the understanding of one's real nature. What we see is not reality, but a projection of our senses. The real is unreal. The unreal is real. The unbroken wholeness is not realised. Enlightenment is surrender of free will and sense of personal identity. Identification has to be there only for the body-mind organism. Instead of identifying with the individual we have to identify with the unbroken wholeness. In an enlightened person the functions of the body and mind mechanism continues without a sense of personal doership. We have to drop the thinking mind and retain the working mind. The basis of this understanding is the radical vision of transcendence. The person or the individual does not really exist. There is only impersonal happiness and individuals don't have free will."

Balsekar says, "There is really no individual. All that exists is consciousness; the original Ground of all Being. Turn inward and become a seeker of Enlightenment. Finally even the *guru* and disciple get merged. When the thinking mind is absent and only the working mind exists, the body, mind organism are no longer in trouble. Be a witness to all actions. All actions are part of totality and not mine. "I" really don't exist. The real "I" is God, the cosmic source."

This education gives me inner security and I start dis-identifying myself with my thoughts and action; becoming more a witness. Gradually I see the sense of doership disappearing.

I listen to the lectures of Swami Ranganathananda of the Ramakrishna Mutt at Natham Road in Madurai. He is very old but soaked in the teachings of Ramakrishna Paramahamsa and it is as though the saint was speaking through this monk. He speaks with full conviction that Ramakrishna's Vedanta is essential for the salvation of humanity. He is happy to learn that my ancestor's *guru*, Paramahamsa Shivahari knew Ramakrishna. Swami Ranganathanandaji, when he heard my description of Shivahari, quotes from the *Brihadaranyaka Upanishad*, "*tatra pita apita bhravati, mata amata, lokah aloka, veda avedah, deva adeva bhavatih* (for the man who has got the highest realisation, his mother ceases to become his mother, his father ceases to become his father, his country ceases to become his country, the Vedas cease to become his Vedas, his gods and goddesses cease to become his gods and goddesses. He becomes a cosmic man)." Swamiji radiates knowledge and I am drawn to him. I admire the way in which he meditates before each lecture, transmitting joy. He quotes Ramakrishna:

"Do you know, of what kind is the meditation of a *jnani*? It is like a bird flying freely in the sky, its joy is boundless." His speeches remind me of how blissful knowledge of the self can be, *satyam jnanam anantam brahma* (knowledge is bliss. Knowledge takes us to infinity. Knowledge takes us to God). Here is a *rishi* before me, contented in the self, lecturing on the *Bhagavad-Gita*. He exemplifies the dictum of the *Chhandogya Upanishad*, "In the final realisation, man transcends his body; he becomes a different body and he lives and moves in the divine light of Knowledge." Swamiji quotes to me from the same Upanishad, "Whatever is done through understanding, through faith and through inward meditation that alone becomes charged with the highest energy." He encourages me to concentrate more on *sadhana* and is happy to learn that I am following the path of Ramana Maharshi. I show Swamiji the manuscript of *Tantraloka* with the unfinished commentaries by Shivahari and Subbiah. He looks at them with interest and tells me about the spiritual unity of India. Swamiji tells me about Acharya Sankara's *guru*, Govinda Bhagavadpada, who was a brahmin from Kashmir. In his *purvashrama* he was Chandra Sarma. Chandra Sarma wanted to listen to Patanjali's exposition of the Vyakarana at Chidambaram and was coming to the south. He met Gaudapada at Badrinath. Gaudapada told him that Patanjali's exposition at Chidambaram was over and he would teach him. There was no writing material available and Chandra Sarma scratched his thigh. Using the blood dripping from the thigh, he wrote on the leaves of the tree. The instructions continued for nine days, in which he had no food or sleep. At the end, Sharma tied the wares in a bundle and after bowing to Gaudapada, left the place. While Sharma was with his teacher, Vyasa, the author of the *Brahma-Sutras*, visited him. Sharma, who had become a *sannyasi* with the name Govinda Bhagavadpada, was instructed by Vyasa to go to the bank of the Narmada River and wait for the arrival of Acharya Sankara, who was the incarnation of Lord Shiva. The purpose of Lord Shiva's arrival on earth in the form of Sri Sankara was to write a *Bhashya* on the *Brahma-Sutras*.

"The Upanishads have defined a Paramahamsa thus: That sage who has solely engaged himself in drinking the nectar which is no other than *Brahman*, the nectar which is the outcome of incessant meditation, that sage becomes the greatest of ascetics, Paramahamsa, and a philosopher free of worldly taint, *avadhuta*. But at the sight of him, the whole world becomes consecrated. Even an ignorant man who is devoted to his service becomes liberated.

"Sri Sankara was a *parivrajaka*, ever on the move exemplifying the doctrine of the *Gita* about which he wrote an excellent commentary that a *jnani* has no desires of his own to satisfy and has nothing to gain for himself. He defeated his opponents and established the supremacy of Advaita Vedanta. He set up ten orders of monks, Paramahamsa *parivrajaka*s and established *mutt*s in Shringeri in the south, Puri in the east, Dvaraka in the west and Badrinath in the north, affirming the geographical and cultural unity of India. The *Paramahamsa*s are detached from the world and are called *parivrajaka acharya*s when they teach. A Paramahamsa is above caste, creed and sect.

"Possessed of extraordinary powers this young boy (Sankara), highly intelligent, has worked wonders in the cultural, philosophical and religious fields of Indian life. He lived at a time when there was a philosophical, cultural and religious crisis in the country. Several systems of thought were in conflict with each other. It was at such a time that the mastermind of Sankara set to work to produce unity in the field of religion, culture and philosophy. He sought harmony and integrated conflicting thought systems under the umbrella of Vedanta. Unity was his aim and not uniformity. Unity in diversity. He had firm belief in the rich diversity in the universe of faiths. Diversity, at times, can also lead to chaos. The purpose of all the great thinkers of this country has been to preserve the variety and subordinate it to an overriding unity. It is a federation of faiths that Sankara established through a system based on reason and free discussion designed to appeal to the heart and mind of the people. Since he brought six religions in one fold, he has been called Sanmata-Sthapana Acharya (the teacher who established six religions). Sankara had an intense desire to understand other points of view. He conceived of Bharatavarsha as a whole and even now the temple in which he meditated in Srinagar, the Sankaracharya Temple is venerated by Muslims. His achievements are unparalleled in the history of mankind. In sharp contrast to those heroes who won through the sword, Sankara captured hearts using logical arguments. His spiritual loftiness impressed everyone. He subscribed to a democratic attitude and used the armours of logic, inference and reason to convert people to his views and defeat his intellectual opponents, unlike the democratic leaders of today. In this we are reminded of the Buddha, and Ramana Maharshi. Sankara appealed to both the heart and the intellect of men. We have in Sankara a great intellectual who also commanded the emotional allegiance of the masses. He wrote *bhashyas*, which are very difficult. He also wrote soul stirring devotional hymns."

Swamiji tells me about his days in Karachi before Partition and his lectures on *Bhagavad-Gita* there which was attended even by Muslims. When he learns about my desire to visit Sind, he urges me to make a pilgrimage to Sadhu Belo Temple, in Bukkur Island, on the banks of Indus River. He speaks nostalgically about his Karachi years and his travels by boat over the Indus.

44

In Delhi, my classmate who retired as Finance Secretary, Government of India, helps me to get a visa to visit Sadhu Belo Temple in Sukkur, Sind, Pakistan. It is a tedious process. I take my flight from Mumbai and reach Karachi in four hours. My friend, Suresh Khatri, whom I knew through internet networking sites, arrives at the airport and takes me to his town Umerkot, a Hindu majority area. There are at least 10 temples in the town and Hindus everywhere. Sind is a great laboratory of communal harmony, where we can see *mandir*s and *masjid*s within the same complex. The strong Sufi tradition in Sind has made the Muslims more tolerant there towards other communities in sharp contrast to Punjab and North West Frontier Province where religious extremism reigns. I am informed by my friend, Khatri, about how the country is getting rapidly Islamised, resulting in the insecurity of the Hindu minority. Poor Hindus keep migrating to India, while the well-to-do go abroad. However, in pockets like Umerkot, and Sukkur, Hindus are secure. The next day, I am taken by car to the Sadhu Belo Temple in Bukkur Island in Sukkur. We are taken on a boat through the Indus River and the Sadhu Belo Temple is located in an island over the river. It is a beautiful temple, well maintained and I offer *puja* there. There are sculptures of Hindu deities everywhere in the temple, with the Sindhi God Jhulelal, seen prominently on a pillar. I offer my prayers on the banks of the Indus River and I am reminded of the Rigvedic verses eulogising it. India derives its name from the Indus and Hindu from Sindhu.

gange cha yamune chaiva
godavari sarasvati

narmade sindhu kaveri
jale asmin sannidhim kuru

"We are essentially Sindhus," said Ramachandra Gandhi to me in Delhi. Jawaharlal Nehru called India an "ancient palimpsest" in which several layers of history can be traced. Several cultural streams have merged in it. A recent excavation in Peshawar has revealed the presence of nearly 10 empires in the history of the city. I take with me some water from the Sindhu and board the flight back to Mumbai, deeply regretting that the period of stay is too short for me to see Taxila, in Punjab and Mohenjo-Daro, in Sind.

45

One of the most romantic stories in history is the discovery of Vedanta by the orientalists in the West during the eighteenth and nineteenth centuries. Henry David Thoreau (1817-62) wrote, "In the morning I bathe my intellect in the stupendous and cosmological philosophy of the *Bhagavad-Gita*, since whose composition, years of the gods have elapsed, and in comparison with which our modern world and its literature seem puny and trivial." Thoreau notes that the Christian and Hindu concepts of man are entirely different. The Christian concept sees man as a sinner while Hinduism sees him as potentially divine. He says, "In the Hindu scripture the idea of man is quite illimitable and sublime. There is nowhere a loftier conception of his destiny." Arthur Schopenhauer (1788-1860) states, "From every sentence (of the Upanishads) deep, original and sublime thoughts arise and the whole is pervaded by a high and holy and earnest spirit. In the whole world there is no study so beneficial and as elevating as that of the Upanishads. They are destined sooner or later to become the faith of the people. It (Upanishad) has been the solace of my life and it will be the solace of my death." Emerson (1803-82) states in his diary that the Vedanta is sublime as night and a breathless ocean. It contains every religious sentiment, all the grand ethics which visit in turn each noble poetic mind."

Humbolt (1767-1835) admired the *Bhagavad-Gita* and called it the deepest and loftiest thing the world has to show.

Max Müller wrote to Renan in 1877: "The Upanishads and the Vedanta, if looked into seriously, contain, I believe, the solution of many difficulties which perplex our philosophy. Only it is not enough to translate them, they require the shoulder of a Christopher to carry them over the channel of 2000 years that runs between the old *vanaprastha*s and us."

Mark Twain (1835-1910) calls India, "land of religions, cradle of human race, birthplace of human speech, grandmother of tradition." He also says, "India has two million gods, and worships them all. In religion all other countries are paupers, India is the only millionaire. And India had the start of the whole world in the beginning of things. She had the first civilisation, she had the first accumulation of material wealth; she was populous with deep thinkers and subtle intellect; she had mines, and woods and a fruitful soul."

Arnold Toynbee (1889-1975) states, "At this supremely dangerous moment in human history, the only way of salvation is the ancient Hindu way." He states elsewhere, "In 50 years, the world would be under the hegemony of the USA, but in the twenty-first century, as religion captures the place of technology, it is possible that India the conquered will conquer its conquerors." Annie Besant (1847-1933) states: "After a study of some 40 years and more of the great religions of the world, I find none so perfect, none so scientific, none so philosophical and none so spiritual than that great religion known by the name of Hinduism. Without Hinduism India has no future. Hinduism is the soil in which India's roots are stuck and torn out of that she will inevitably wither as a tree torn from its place. And if Hindus do not maintain Hinduism, who shall save it? If India's children do not cling to her faith who shall guard it? India alone can save India and India and Hinduism are one." Annie Besant remarks in Calcutta: "India is the mother of religions. In her are combined science and religion in perfect harmony, and that is the Hindu religion, and it is India that shall be again the spiritual mother of the world." Paul Deussen (1845-1919) has also praised India in eloquent terms. In a lecture he delivered in Bombay in 1893 he said:

> On the tree of Indian wisdom there is no greater flower than the Upanishads, and no finer fruit than the Vedanta philosophy. This system grew out of the teachings of the Upanishads and was brought to its consummate form by the great Sankara (born CE 788, exactly 1,000 years before his spiritual kinsman Schopenhauer). Even to this day, Sankara's system represents the common belief of nearly all thoughtful Hindus and deserves to be widely studied in the occident.

Romain Rolland (1866-1944), the French Nobel prize winner in Literature, has won the hearts of several generations with his biography of Vivekananda and was deeply influenced by Vedanta. Dara Shikoh (1615-59), the elder brother of Aurangzeb, translated the Upanishads from Sanskrit to Persian and it was this translation which inspired Sir William Jones (1746-94), the great orientalist, to study the Indian classics. The founder of Indology was Alberuni (973-1048), who accompanied Mohammed Ghazni, and studied Sanskrit. He has given us a scholarly book on India during the tenth century.

The most inspiring Indologist to me is Ji Xianlin (1911-) who is nearly 85 years old at the time of writing. He is a former professor of Eastern Studies at Peking University. He has led a disciplined life, getting up at 4.30 in the morning and studies Sanskrit and Pali texts. He secretly translated the *Ramayana* from Sanskrit into Chinese in poetic form, during the period of the Cultural Revolution when intellectuals were persecuted. He has written several books on India and is fully devoted to Sanskrit literature. He has a self-effacing nature and is spartan in his habits. He is a monument of learning in Indology. I regret that I do not have the resources to travel to China and meet this legend of Indology.

However, my meeting with Professor Vishnu Bhatt, in the Madras Christian College, Madras, compensates for this. He looks like the *pandit*s of yore and is immersed in Sanskritic scholarship. He says, "Everything was based on *dharma* in ancient India. These days everyone is after money. The humanitarian movements of the eighteenth century made everything man-centric," he says. "The Vedic *rishi*s did not reveal their names. The ego was considered a big barrier. Though Sri Sankara wrote innumerable works, he did not write anything about himself. Modern urban development is chaotic. Research has to be done on the *sabha* system and how rural self-governance worked efficiently for centuries.

"The *varna dharma* removed the greatest evil called money. The brahmin was not allowed to touch money. If brahmins are suffering now, they themselves are responsible for it. Why did they give up the teaching of the Vedas?" He feels the Indians are losing their direction by embracing Western modes of thought and lifestyle, seeking comforts. Ancient India concentrated on the self. In the name of progress we are abandoning age-old values and the focus is now on the individual and the result is the Western man-centric vision. Thus we see violence, fragile relationships, breakdown of joint family system and overall loss of peace in the society. Unless we go back to our roots, we are doomed as a nation.

Professor Vishnu Bhat tells me about Uttaramerur near Kanchipuram, where there was an electoral system and a written constitution 1,300 years ago. The village assembly (*grama sabha*) administered the village perfectly and the corrupt had no place in the system. All these details are meticulously noted on the walls of the village assembly (*grama sabha mandapa* which was in the *mandapa* of the Vaikuntaperumal Temple). The Pallava king Nandivarman II established it around CE 750 and the village has a 1,300-year history.

"This inscription, dated around CE 920 in the reign of Paraantaka Chola, is an outstanding document in the history of India, notes R. Nagaswamy, former Director, Tamil Nadu Department of Archaeology. "It is a veritable written

Constitution of the village assembly that functioned 1,000 years ago," Nagaswamy says in his book, *Uthiramerur, the Historic Village in Tamil Nadu*. The book has been published by the Tamil Arts Academy, Chennai.

Dr Nagaswamy writes: "It [the inscription] gives astonishing details about the constitution of wards, the qualification of candidates standing for elections, the disqualification norms, the mode of election, the constitution of committees with elected members, the functions of [those] committees, the power to remove the wrong-doer, etc.

"On the walls of the *mandapa* are inscribed a variety of secular transactions of the village, dealing with administrative, judicial, commercial, agricultural, transportation and irrigation regulations, as administered by the then village assembly, giving a vivid picture of the efficient administration of the village society in the bygone ages. The villagers even had the right to recall the elected representatives if they failed in their duty." The wrong doers, including village administrators, were punished. Democratic participation extended to a large section of the society. During the assembly meeting it was compulsory for everyone, including women and children, to attend them. Only the invalid and those who had gone on pilgrimages were exempted. In the Vedic college of the village, the teacher had to be appointed from outside (the native of the soil is likely to be lenient to the students) and the scholarship required for the post was very high unlike our times. This is just one of the innumerable village assemblies that existed in Tamil Nadu for centuries, until the arrival of the British.

The stunning revelations of Dharampal, who studied documents of the East India Company in London, that Indians were highly advanced in all spheres and education was widespread in the society cutting across caste lines before the arrival of the British call the bluff of the propaganda of British historians who depicted India as a backward country before their arrival. He proves with evidence that during the eighteenth century 80 per cent of students studying in schools in Tamil Nadu were from backward castes.

46

SUBRAMANIA Bharati, in his autobiography, severely condemned the modern brahmins who, with his English education, worked as officials in the service of the foreign ruler and aped the white man's ways. Bharati condemned "this degraded Kaliyuga when the brahmin community has become degraded." The Tamil writer Jeyakanthan in his essay, "Why I am a Brahmin" said that India gained eminence in the past due to *varnashrama dharma* and its disappearance has led to decline of values. He further said that Brahminism was a status that could be attained by anyone and pointed out that some of the finest *rishi*s like Vishvamitra (a *brahmarshi*) were not brahmin by birth. Through spirituality, Indian civilisation gained full splendour. In the olden days the brahmin clung on to *unchavritti* as his *dharma* and won the admiration and respect of rest of the society. Even the Jain author of *Silappadikaram*, Ilango Adigal, makes Kannaki say, "Let the city (Madurai) burn except brahmins and cows." After the colonial period fissures developed in the Hindu society; it is necessary now to forget the past 400 years of cultural degeneration and revive the ancient glory of India when people lived in harmony.

Vallalar Ramalingaswami, the great saint from Tamil Nadu, preached Universal Brotherhood and his *mantra*s *Jivakarunyam*, compassion to all living beings and *Thaniperumkarunai*, supreme compassion, are eternally relevant. We have to create a new society based on the teachings of Vallalar, Sri Aurobindo, Ramana Maharshi, Ramakrishna Paramahamsa, Vivekananda, Narayana Guru and Mahatma Gandhi. Sri Aurobindo in *Life Divine* states that a new race of Supermen will emerge taking us to higher levels of consciousness. The human being is, he says, a laboratory in which God consciousness is being experimented. We have emerged from *Satchidananda* and are moving towards *Satchidananda*. We have to raise our consciousness and realise the Divine in us. The French philosopher and Jesuit priest Pierre Teilhard de Chardin states that we are not human beings having a spiritual experience but spiritual beings having a human experience. We are spiritual beings, eternal, all-powerful. This is similar to the Advaitic idea that we are essentially God going through a human experience and not man going through a God experience.

47

I AM in Srinagar, climbing the footsteps of the Sankaracharya Temple in the Takht-e-Suleiman Hills. Acharya Sankara meditated in this temple during his visit to Kashmir. Kashmir was the headquarters of studies on the Veda and Tantra in India until the thirteenth century. Alberuni, when he visited India, observes that *pandit*s who were attacked by Ghazni's army fled to Kashmir. Non-Hindus were not allowed to enter the state in those days, and hence Alberuni was denied entry. He describes the popularity of the Sharada Peeth, now in Pakistan occupied Kashmir, in those times. I meditate before the *Shivalinga,* in an atmosphere permeated by the sonorous chants of the *pandit.* It is a Srinagar overshadowed by militancy, far different from the land which Acharya Sankara visited during the late seventh or early eighth century CE. Terrorists from Pakistan cross the Line of Control and enter the state, creating mayhem. Srinagar is under curfew for two days and I stay in my hotel. I visit the Sankaracharya temple again, when the curfew is lifted. I am filled with admiration for the young Sri Sankara who won debates here. Acharya Sankara's visit to Kashmir is an eloquent testimony to his belief in the spiritual and cultural unity of India. Study of the Tantra made the soil fertile for the arrival of Acharya Utpala and Acharya Abhinavagupta. This was the same Kashmir which was visited by the *guru* of Paramahamsa Shivahari. The *guru* had done tantric *sadhana* at Kheer Bhawani Temple and the Divine Mother, appearing before him, had given *darshan* to him. I also take a taxi and worship at Kheer Bhawani Temple.

The great tradition of Kashmiri Shaivism ended with the death of Swami Lakshman Joo in 1992 and terrorism now sucks the life blood of the people. The *pandit*s of Kashmir have also left the valley and many of them have been murdered by terrorists. The tragedy of the Kashmiri *pandit*s awaits its Aeschylus. The massacre of the *pandit*s by Pakistan-trained terrorists has led to the total migration of the community to other parts of India and an entire generation has grown up outside the valley with no idea about their homeland. An entire generation of Kashmiri Muslims has also grown up without any contacts with their *pandit* brethren. Living in tents in Delhi, the *pandit*s survive in abysmal conditions, living in nostalgia about olden days. The *jehad* against the Hindus of Kashmir unleashed by the neighbouring country has resulted in long-term damage to the secular character of the Kashmir Valley, and harmonious co-existence of Hindus and Muslims has become a thing of the past.

Politics apart, I admire the scenic beauty of the Valley and visit temples. The hotel receptionist discourages me from visiting the Marttand Temple in north Kashmir, "Too much violence there. Don't go, sir," he tells me. I spend my last day in Srinagar at the Sankaracharya Temple, imagining the days when kings patronised the saint scholar from the south. I think about the days when scholars congregated here discussing the intricacies of the Shastras. The grandeur of nature here kindled in the minds of the saints of the Valley the need to raise their levels of consciousness in the form of Tantra and realise that they were Shiva Himself. The presence of Bhairava can be felt everywhere. I am enthralled to discover that Sufism is still surviving in the Valley and the militants have not been successful in talibanising the Valley. Perhaps, the spirit of Sankaracharya will save the State from collapse and the good old days of harmony will return. I recollect the words of André Malraux to Jawaharlal Nehru in Paris (1936), "Europe is destructive, suicidal. Europe, like Nietzsche understood, and who understood Europe better than Nietzsche, is a cemetery of ideas. Yes, we cannot go beyond good and evil. We can never go, as the Indians can, beyond duality. India had Sankara." Malraux's parting words to Nehru are, "Keep India from duality. Let the great Sankaracharya, let him guide India. Such is my prayer."

The Vyasa *parampara* has kept the Vedantic tradition alive in India and a series of Vyasas have appeared to add new life to Sanatana Dharma. The writings of S. Radhakrishnan can inspire people from all walks of life to appreciate the richness of our tradition and its amazing resilience. I am attracted to the seductive flow of words in the works of this great philosopher whose vision is all-encompassing and far-sighted like that of the Vedic *rishi*s. His undying enthusiasm for the spiritual and economic upliftment of Indians based on the foundations laid by the seers of the Upanishads should be our goal. Another sage whose works I keep revisiting is Sri Aurobindo, a Vyasa of our times, about whom if I were to elaborate, it would take an entire book. Sri Aurobindo felt that Sayana's version of the Vedas written in the fourteenth century was a literal translation of the verses and he has given us a mystical interpretation of this spiritual classic. A study of the works of Sri Aurobindo, Swami Vivekananda and S. Radhakrishnan can help the young people to remain rooted in our tradition and develop pride in our cultural values. They were never prisoners of a foreign idiom.

I make a pilgrimage to Kamarpukur, the serene village in Bengal, where Ramakrishna was born. I also go to Kalady and Veliyanad in Kerala, two places associated with the birth of Sri Sankara. At Veliyanad village near Ernakulam, Chinmaya Mission runs an International Research Centre (called Adi Sankara Nilayam) in Vedanta, conducting several spiritual camps. Swami Advayanandaji, the youthful and ebullient Swamiji in charge of the place is extremely hospitable and I attend a camp on *Vivekachudamani* conducted by Swami Sivayoganandaji. Swamini Niranjanandaji, lovingly called *Amma* by everyone, clears several doubts of mine about Vedanta.

Acharya Sankara says in *Vivekachudamani*:

> The affirmation (of the theist) that God is, and the negation (of the atheist) that God is not, both these are nothing but pulsations of *buddhi*; it never touches the eternal Reality (behind the buddhi).

This is the most scientific statement on God. This idea that God is the self of even the atheist made India the land of communal harmony and the reason behind the tolerance of the Hindus towards other religions and diverse schools of thought.

48

I RETURN to Madurai and my normal schedule of visiting Ramana Kendra continues. My study of the life of Subbiah and Paramahamsa Shivahari gives me tremendous inner happiness. Sankara Shastri's classes on Acharya Sankara have also given a new purpose in my life. This has made me love creation. "God is the supreme *kavi*," said Chaitanya Mahaprabhu. The creator is a *rasajna*, a Knower of enjoyment. The universe is a *lila* of God, as Subbiah's father once told him. God is *rasa, rasovai*. He is Himself enjoyment; He enjoys our enjoyment of the universe. It is our destiny to evolve from *Sisupti* to Shivahood. We descent into an animal state when we forget this evolutionary process. Our true nature is *Satchidananda*. Advaita, wrote K. Swaminathan, teaches us that, "all life is holy, all selves are one self and God is not wholly other." Muruganaar said, "Destroy the false duality of this world and that world. Seeing the true oneness of all and being the joy of right awareness; this alone is Shivahood." Mahamahopadhyaya Swaminatha Iyer once said to Bhagavan Ramana Maharshi, "People tell me to give up *patru* (attachment). But I am not able to give up Tamil *patru*." Bhagavan replied, "But who asked you to give up Shiva *patru* or Tamil *patru*?" K. Swaminathan wrote, "What is Shiva but poetry, the creator and creation of *ananda*?"

My head is full of the journeys of Subbiah and Shivahari, Neelakanta Dikshitar and Appaya Dikshitar, Sadashiva Brahmendra and Upanishad Brahmachari; Kumaraguruparar and Ramalingaswamy, Acharya Sankara and Acharya Govindapada; Acharya Abhinavagupta and other Kashmiri luminaries. My reading of Manikkavacakar, Vallalar Ramalingaswamy, and Muruganaar makes me feel proud of

Tamil culture with its historic temples and ancient tradition. The kings who ruled Tamil country patronised the Vedas making Subramania Bharati write, *vedam niraintha tamilnadu* (a State where Vedas flourish). Temple inscriptions in Tamil Nadu are full of references to tax-free lands (*chatur vedamangalams*) given by kings to Vedic brahmins. In a deed of Karikala Chola, he describes himself as the enemy of those who did not follow Veda Shastra. A king of the Sangam Age was known by the name "Pal Yagasalai Mudhu Kudumi Peruvazhudhi" (referring to the *yajnas* performed during his reign). A Professor remarked that his study of *Manusmriti* has made him lose enthusiasm for buying the latest book published abroad. Friedrich Nietzsche said: "Close the Bible and open the *Manusmriti*. It has an affirmation of life, a triumphing, agreeable sensation in life and that to draw up a lawbook such as Manu means to permit oneself to get the upper hand, to become perfection, to be ambitious of the highest art of living." In the *Bhagavatam* it is stated that Manu, the author of *Manusmriti*, was a king who lived near the Vaigai River; Vedic *dharma* was born here. The Puranas state that Kalki *avatara* will be born as the son to a Vedic brahmin in the Tirunelveli region of Dravida Nadu. Nattukotai Chettiars and Vellalars established Veda *pathashalas* throughout the Tamil country. Avvaiyar said, "Do not allow even one day to pass without *Odhal* (*veda adhyayana*)." A great university was established in Kanchipuram, when Kashmir fell to the sword of Islam, where Tamilians taught Sanskrit and Pali texts. In Vedic scholarship Kanchipuram was second only to Varanasi in India. Even Patanjali, in his *Mahabhashya*, mentions the achievements of the scholars at Kanchi. Tinganaga the progenitor of Tarka Shastra (logic) was a Tamilian. Pandurang Vaman Kane's *History of Dharmashastras*, running to nearly 7,000 pages, informs us that the Indian Constitution has given the false opinion to the people that they have rights but no obligations, unlike our Dharmashastra which laid stress on duties. We have broken away from the traditional ideas prevalent in India and as a result we see confusion everywhere. At the *agrahaaram* in Brahmadesham, while admiring the *Kartikai* lights, I ruminate on the future of the Vedic tradition. The street has a dozen brahmins who are extremely hospitable. The term *agrahaaram* means a garland of houses leading to a temple. A typical *agrahaaram* house, with *kolams* in the front, contains the following rooms, *Thinnai, pyol,* Rezhi, an entrance to the house, Muttram, open area used for performance of *yajnas*, Paththayam, storeroom, Samayal Kattu, kitchen, and Kollai, backyard, which has a *tulasi* plant for worship. Each section of the house was constructed in order to maintain the spiritual way of living. In these houses *agnihotra* was maintained permanently and Vedas were recited daily. The *pandit* (*ganapadigal*) in the street shows me an abandoned building, which was once a *pathashala,* where he taught *Rigveda*. This village was once the headquarters of Vedic Studies in the area. Raja-Raja Chola had gifted acres of lands (*chaturvedamangalams*) for the promotion of Vedas and *yajnas* with Brahmadesham as capital. There was a powerful *mahasabha* which governed several such villages in this place meticulously. Probably this is only a transitory period and the collective genius of Bharatavarsha will recognise the necessity of atmic quest.

Tiruvalluvar wrote the *Kural* and went to Madurai for presenting it to a group of scholars for approval. He placed the work on a wooden plank floating on the lotus pond of Meenakshi Temple. The work remained on the plank while productions of other poets sank. Several poets praised the work. A poet said, "I thought about it, whether Sanskrit is superior or Tamil. Both Sanskrit and Tamil are equal. It cannot be said that one is superior and the other is inferior. This is because there is Veda in Sanskrit and in Tamil, *Tirukural,* has come now. This is the Tamil *Marai* (Veda)." It was in this culture that Thayumanavar and Pattinathar appeared. Ramalingaswamy has given us the path to a new spiritual renaissance.

In Ramanathapuram at the Muruganaar Kendra, I talk to a relative of the local *zamindar* who assures me that Sanatana Dharma is eternal. Children, women, elders from all castes and classes congregate at the Kendra singing *bhajans*. Muruganaar belonged to Ramanathapuram, and surrendered completely to Bhagavan Ramana Maharshi, composing some of the finest poetry in Tamil in praise of his *guru*. At the *agrahaaram* in Ramanathapuram, where there are still a few Sanskrit *pandits*, I dream of Taxila, Kashmir, Gandhara and the continuity of India's intellectual and spiritual traditions. I admire the spiritual and intellectual zeal that made a scholar, Madhuraja, from Madurai travel to Kashmir in the eleventh century to meet the great Abhinavagupta. What Higher force led the great Sankara to meet Acharya Govinda, a Kashmiri brahmin, in the Narmada Valley? The Divine Mother, be it Meenakshi in Madurai or Sharada in Kashmir, guides mortals to carry out the scheme of the Divine. Meenakshi led Ramana Maharshi to Arunachala and Sharada made Abhinavagupta compose immortal works. Meenakshi made Mahatma Gandhi abandon Western dress and take to *khadi* in Madurai. The Goddess attracts pilgrims from all over the world, radiating Her effulgence to the mighty and low. It is to the same Meenakshi that Shivahari and Subbiah surrendered. I pray to Her everyday to grant me self-realisation. Madurai is my Kashi, my Jerusalem. An individual becomes twice-born (*dvija*) when he or she realises the self and the *yajnopavitam* (sacred thread) symbolises the individual's resolve to get into self-enquiry. The *yajnopavitam* will survive all the bashing of our age-old traditions that we see in contemporary times. Though the Tamil Nadu has gone through the trauma of atheistic movements which ridiculed Hindu gods and goddesses and conducted procession of idols of gods garlanded with *chappals*, the temples are now overflowing with devotees from all castes. India was created by the Divine for spirituality alone and people with interest for matters of the spirit, tired of the sensuous world, will always come to Bharatavarsha to quench their thirst. "India is not a *desha*, but a *darsana*,"said Raja Rao. India stands for things eternal. India is an idea, a metaphysic, for this legendary Indian writer. *Sat-chit-ananda* is the foundation on which ancient Indians achieved a lot in arts, music, architecture, poetry, drama. All human activities are sacred for us and we see a divine spark in everyone. He wrote: "Whether it is through Dante or Shakespeare, through St. Thomas Aquinas or Nietzsche, you come back to the Upanishads and the Vedanta, realising that wheresoever you go, you always return to the Himalayas, and whatever the rivers that flow, the waters are of the Gangotri." We, Indians, clung on to our inner spiritual resources during the inferno of Islamic invasion, which no other nation could have survived, and forgave those who vandalised our magnificent temples. The British rule was another horrible chapter in our history. The Christian missionaries were openly encouraged by the rulers to convert the local population. Despite all this, Sanatana Dharma survived.

As I enjoy watching the Samavedic chanting of boys with tufts in a Veda *pathashala* inside Tiruparamkundram Temple of Lord Subrahmanya, all tensions related to my wife and daughter disappear. The "I" disappears and the self takes its place. Abhinavagupta contributed the concept of *shanta rasa* about which he wrote in his *Locana,* a commentary on Anandavardhana's *Dhvanyaloka. Shanta rasa,* he said, "is the ultimate end of art. All emotions, when their exciting conditions are present emerge from *shanta,* and when these conditions are withdrawn they again merge into *shanta.*"

Acknowledgement

THE following books have been consulted for the writing of this book. For the quotations from Upanishads, *Vivekachudamani*, *Ribhu Gita* and *Atma-Bodha* the books published by Advaita Ashram (Mayavati); Ramakrishna Mission (Calcutta) and S. Radhakrishnan's *The Principal Upanishads* (Harper Collins) have been used. The quotations from *Madurai Kanchi* is from *The Wonder That Was India* by A.L. Basham (Rupa & Co). The quotation of *Manisha Panchakam* is from Swami Ranganathananda's book, *Sankaracharya and an Untouchable: An Exposition of Manisha Panchakam* (Advaita Ashrama). Some sections of the spiritual experiences of Paramahamsa Shivahari are based on the biographical and autobiographical accounts of Ramakrishna Paramahamsa, Swami Vivekananda, T.V. Kapali Sastriar and Sri Abhinava Vidyatheerta Mahaswamigal of Sringeri. Ji Xianlin, the Chinese Indologist, died on 11 July 2009. The books of Gurudev Swami Chinmayanandji, Swami Krisnanandji (Divine Life Society) and Swami Ranganathanandji (Ramakrishna Mutt) have been a perennial source of inspiration to me. I bow to them and also to the *rishi*s of Bharatavarsha.

Bibliography

Abhinavagupta, *Sri Tantralokah* (2 vols): tr. Gautam Chatterjee, Varanasi, Indian Mind, 2008.

Annamalai, S., "Neglect Wrecks a Nayak Legacy" *The Hindu*, http://www.hinduon net.com/thehindu/thscrip/print.pl?file= 2007041919050500.htm &date= 2007/04/19/

Ashokananda, Swami, *Avadhuta Gita of Dattatreya*, Calcutta: Ramakrishna Mission.

Aspects of Vedanta, Calcutta: Ramakrishna Mission.

Bamzai, P.N.K., "Kashmir: The Home of Sanskrit Language and Literature" (*Hinduism Today*, Issue 94-03).

Chandrasekharendra Saraswati, *Acharya's Call* (Part 1 &2), Madras Discourses, Chennai, Sri Kamakoti Peetam, 1995.

Chandrasekharendra Saraswati, *Hindu Dharma*, Bharatiya Vidya Bhavan.

Chandrasekharendra Saraswati, *Voice of God* (vol. I) Mumbai, Sri Kanchi, Mahaswami Peetarohana Satabdi Mahotsava Trust, 2009.

Chaudhuri, Nirad. C, *Scholar Extraordinary*, Delhi, Oxford University Press, London, 1974.

Desai, Morarji, *The Story of My Life*, 3 vols, New Delhi, S. Gowri & Company Ltd., 1979.

Dhar, K.N., "Abhinavagupta: The Philosopher."

Dhar, K.N., *Kalhana: The Chronicle.*

Eastern and Western, *The Life of Swami Vivekananda* Disciples (2 vols), Calcutta: Ramakrishna Mission.

Gambhirananda, Swami, *Chandogya Upanishad,* Calcutta: Ramakrishna Mission.

Gambhirananda, Swami, *Reminiscence of Swami Ranganathananda,* Calcutta: Ramakrishna Mission.

Gambhirananda, Swami, *The Monks Without Frontiers,* Calcutta: Ramakrishna Mission.

Ganesan, V., *Fragrant Pearls (An anthology),* Tiruvannamalai: Ramanasramam.

Ganesan, V., *Moments Remembered: Reminiscences of Bhagavan Ramana,* Tiruvannamalai: Ramanasramam.

Ganesan, V., *The Collected Works of Sri Ramana Maharshi,* 2007, Tiruvannamalai: Ramanasramam.

Godman, David, *Power of the Presence* (Part 2), 2001, Tiruvannamalai: Ramanasramam

The Gospel of Sri Ramakrishna, Calcutta: Ramakrishna Mission.

Gupta, Mahendranath (M), *The Gospel of Sri Ramakrishna,* Calcutta: Ramakrishna Mission.

Jalali, R.K., "Abhinavagupta, — The Encyclopaedic Scholar," *Koshur Samachar.*

Kanagasabai, R., *The Mystical Temple of Meenakshi Sundareswarar,* Madurai, published by the author, 2006.

Kapoor, Kapil, "Decolonising the Indian Mind" Keynote address delivered on 18 February 2001 at the National Seminar on Decolonising English Education, Department of English, North Gujarat University, Patan (Gujarat).

Kapoor, Kapil, "Eleven Objections to Sanskrit Literary Theory: A Rejoinder". http://www.indian science.org/essays/st_es_kapoo_eleven.shtml & www.ifih.org/eleven objectionstoSanskritlLiterarytheory.htm

Kapoor, Kapil, *"Literary Theory : Indian Conceptual Framework,"* Affiliated, East-West Press Private Limited, 1998.

Kapoor, Kapil, "Loss, Recovery and Renewal of Texts in Indian's Tradition."

Kapoor, Kapil, "Theory of Novel: Indian View," *Indian Response to Critical Theory*, Creative Publishers, 1996.

Kaw, R.K., "Shaivism & Kashmir's Doctrine of "Recognition" (*Pratyabhijna*).

Krishnananda, Swami, *Talks on Scriptures*, Rishikesh: Divine Life Society.

Krishnananda, Swami, *Talks on Vedanta*, Rishikesh: Divine Life Society.

Krishnananda, Swami, *The Brihadaranyaka Upanishad*, Rishikesh: Divine Life Society.

Krishnananda, Swami, *The Katha Upanishad*, Rishikesh: Divine Life Society.

Krishnananda, Swami, *The Philosophy of Bhagavadgita*, Rishikesh: Divine Life Society.

Lakshman Joo, Swami (Maharaj), "Acharya Abhinavagupta "Siva incarnate to enlighten the people," *Koshur Samachar*.

Lakshman Joo, Swami (Maharaj), "Kashmir Shaivism."

Lokeswarananda, Swami, *Chandogya Upanishad*, Calcutta: Ramakrishna Mission.

Madhavananda, Swami, *The Brihadaranyaka Upanishad*, Calcutta: Ramakrishna Mission.

Mascaro, Juan, *The Upanishads*, United Kingdom: Penguin Classics, 1965.

Menon, Keshava, *The Mind of Adi Sankaracharya*, New Delhi, Jaico Books, 1996.

Menon, Ramesh, *The Mahabharata*: *A Modern Rendering* (2 vols.), Delhi, Rupa, 2005.

Mudaliar, Devaraja, *Day by Day with Bhagavan*, Tiruvannamalai: Ramanasramam.

Mukhyananda, Swami, *Life & Philosophy of Sri Sankaracharya*, Calcutta: Ramakrishna Mission.

Muruganaar, *Sri Ramana Anubhuti* (trs. Robert Butler), 1948, Tiruvannamalai: Ramanasramam.

Nandakumar, Prema, *T.V. Kapali Sastriar*, Delhi, Munshiram Manoharlal Publisher Pvt. Ltd., 1998.

Narsimha Swami, B.V., *Self-Realisation*, Tiruvannamalai: Ramanasramam.

Neelakandair, Aravindan. S, Mandapam Ruins of Kanyakumari District: An Overview, as Part of Fellowship Project awarded by Dept. of Culture, Govt. of India.

Nikhilananda, Swami, *Man in Search of Immortality*, Calcutta: Ramakrishna Mission.

Nikhilananda, Swami, *Self-Knowledge (Atma-Vidya), of Sri Sankaracharya*, 2008, Calcutta: Ramakrishna Mission.

Nikhilananda, Swami, *Talks with Swami Vivekananda*, Calcutta: Ramakrishna Mission.

Pandit, M.P., *Life Beautiful*, Pondicherry: Dipti Publication.

Pandit, M.P., *Versatile Genius: Sri T.V. Kapali Sastriar*, Pondicherry: Dipti Publication.

Paranjape, Makarand, "Decolonising English Studies: Attaining Swaraj," Valedictory Address — Department of English, North Gujarat University, Patan (Gujarat).

Ranganathananda, Swami, *Practical Vedanta and the Science of Values*, 2008, Calcutta: Ramakrishna Mission.

Ranganathananda, Swami, *Universal Message of the Bhagavad-Gita* (3 vols.), Calcutta: Ramakrishna Mission.

Rao, Raja, *The Meaning of India*, Delhi: Vision Books.

Saradananda, Swami, *Sri Ramakrishna: The Great Master*, Calcutta: Ramakrishna Mission.

Sankaracharya, *Enlightening Expositions*.

Sankaracharya, *Life and Teachings of His Holiness Jagadguru Sri Abhinava Vidyathirtha Mahaswamigal*.

Sankaracharya, *Personification of Perfection*, 2002.

Sankaracharya, *Sankara: The Missionary*, 2008, Mumbai: Central Chinmaya Mission Trust.

Sankaracharya, *Yoga, Enlightenment and Perfection*, Sri Abhinava Vidyathirtha Mahaswamigal, 2008.

Shraddhananda, Swami, *Seeing God Everywhere*, 1998, Calcutta: Ramakrishna Mission.

Subramanian, K., *Uniqueness of Sri Bhagavan*, Tiruvannamalai: Ramanasramam.

Suri, Nagamma, *Letters from Sri Ramanasramam*, 2008, Tiruvannamalai: Ramanasramam.

Swamiji, Paramananda, Bharati, *Foundations of Dharma*, Bangalore: Jnana-samvardhani Pratishthanam, 2008.

Swaminathan, K., *Sri Ramana, The Self Supreme*, 1997, Tiruvannamalai: Ramanasramam.

Swaminathan, K., *Surpassing Love and Grace : An Offering from His Devotees*, 2001, Tiruvannamalai: Ramanasramam.

Tagare, G.V., *The Pratyabhijna Philosophy*, Delhi: Motilal Banarsidass Publishers, 2002.

Tathagatananda, Swami, *The Basic Ideas of Hinduism and How it is Transmitted*, The Vedanta Society of New York, 2009, Calcutta: Ramakrishna Mission.

Tirumantiram, Calcutta: Ramakrishna Mission.

Tirumular (Trs. B. Natarajan), Calcutta: Ramakrishna Mission.

Venkataramiah, Munagala, *Talks with Sri Ramana Maharshi*, 2008, Tiruvannamalai: Ramanasramam.

Warrier, A.G, Krishna, *Bhagavad Gita Bhashya of Sankaracharaya*, Calcutta: Ramakrishna Mission.

Notes

(1) Dr Premanandakumar's essay available on the website on Kodaganallur village and essay on Neelakanta Dikshitar at www.pallamadai.com were consulted.

(2) The quotations by the Indologists have been taken from www.hinduwisdom.info/quotes41_60.htm.

(3) For information on Kashmir Shaivism the following articles in the website of Kashmir Overseas Association www.kouusa.org/shaivism have been consulted:

Index